STOCKPORT

history & guide

STOCKPORT

history & guide

Steve Cliffe

TEMPUS

First published 2005

Tempus Publishing Limited
The Mill, Brimscombe Port,
Stroud, Gloucestershire, GL5 2QG
www.tempus-publishing.com

British Library Cataloguing in Publication Data.
A catalogue record for this book is available from the British Library.

ISBN 0 7524 3525 6

Typesetting and origination by Tempus Publishing Limited
Printed in Great Britain

Contents

Acknowledgements

This book would never have seen the light of day had it not been for the IT expertise of my patient friend, Bill Hoad. Thanks also to Jim Clare and Grace Collier who loaned their pictures from the Heritage Centre collection. Talented artist David Kelsall allowed me to use his historic paintings of past scenes and Stockport Local Heritage librarian David Reid gave permission for use of Stockport Library pictures and read the proofs. Frank Galvin supplied other historic photographs from SMBC Heritage Services and Alison Farthing of SMBC Tourism & Marketing Unit also helped. My long-time colleague Peter Arrowsmith assisted with information, as did Neil Winstanley of Lithaprint, Manchester Local Studies Library, GMAU/UMAU, Marple Local History Society and Mellor Archaeological Trust. If I have missed anyone, please accept my sincere apologies. Finally, I am indebted to Sandra for insisting that I ought to write it, when I was merely trifling agreeably with the idea.

Stockport Market Place in 1800 with the old church, which was demolished and rebuilt in 1813 after bell-ringing weakened the tower. Staircase House is to the left, butchers' shops in the middle, and the Old Rectory beyond. The scene would have been familiar to Bonnie Prince Charlie, who passed through with his troops half a century before.

Introduction

Stockport is a town with an ancient past, so the vast amount of available information must of necessity be limited within the scope of a short history and guide of this nature. I make no apology therefore for being selective in my choice of subjects. Although chronological in some degree, they reflect my interest and 'take' on particular aspects of history. Remembering the old adage that 'history is a myth generally agreed upon', I have to add that historians are continually reassessing old myths and inventing new ones, particularly local historians, and as for archaeologists, well! However, there are a fair number of facts we can be confident of. From the microlithic fragments of a Stone Age culture, through Bronze Age urns, Roman coins and tiles, medieval stones, earthenware and documents – not forgetting a living medieval church and on through industrial ages to the present air and motorway-borne age – we trace the evolution of modern Stockport.

For the past eighteen years I have edited *Stockport Heritage*, a local magazine dealing with local history and conservation. Thanks to overwhelming interest and contributions from members of the reading public, I am always learning new things about Stockport. I hope that by reading this book, you may too.

Stephen Cliffe, Ridge End, Marple
Spring 2005

Chapter 1

Early History

The landscape of Stockport is varied and interesting, reflecting its underlying geology – scoured by four rivers and numerous tributary brooks and bounded by hills. The Mersey Valley contains significant glacial terraces of sands and gravels on which sit the townships of Gatley and Cheadle, Heaton Mersey and Heaton Norris. Most of the rest of the town is overlaid by heavy boulder clay, with a few hollows that formed mosslands at Great Moor and Kitts Moss, Bramhall.

In the east, coal-bearing rocks outcrop in the rising foothills of the Pennines, while in the west the Permo-Triassic red sandstone gives the lower Goyt and Tame Valleys and the Mersey gorge through the town centre its characteristic rocky appearance.

Long before a bustling town of today's proportions could ever be conceived of, when the lower valleys were clothed with impassable swamp and tangled forest, early people made their home on the eastern fringes of the borough on a cleared hilltop at Mellor.

We are fortunate that recent excavations have revealed more about life in Stockport at this period. It was believed that human activity began here in the Middle Stone Age or Mesolithic period of 8000 to 3500 BC – that is, about 10,000 years ago. Flint arrowheads and scrapers left by these people on the sites of seasonal camps, showing how they followed the migration of game in this period after the last Ice Age, have been found mainly in the Pennine uplands. Flint flakes and blades of Mesolithic date, possibly imported from the Yorkshire or Lincolnshire wolds, or the nearer Trent Valley, have been recovered from the dig beside the Old Rectory on the hilltop at Mellor. This implies the site was first used as a summer hunting base in the Peaks.

It is reasonable to suppose that the Goyt, Tame and Mersey Valleys also supported seasonal hunting groups. The natural crevices in the sandstone left by the glacial melt waters could be easily hollowed out into caves by early man using bone, antler or tools of stone to provide shelters in the soft friable rock.

Cobden Edge rises up above Strines Valley near Marple on the eastern fringe of the borough. Here, and at Mellor nearby, the earliest evidence for human activity has been found: remains of burial mounds, a 14cm-long flint dagger, pottery and a camp on the gritstone edge of the Pennines. A reconstructed hut at Mellor is pictured above.

These riverside caves exist in several places: at Woodbank, with excellent views of the wide and fertile Goyt Valley, near Mersey Street in Portwood, beside Tin Brook on the Underbanks, and in the cliffs overlooking the river at Brinksway, below the present road. Their age has never been determined and excavations have yet to be carried out, but a dig in similar cave shelters on the Etherow at Broadbottom in Tameside yielded evidence of millennia of occupation.

At Mellor, as elsewhere in the borough, archaeological evidence from the succeeding New Stone Age or Neolithic period has also been uncovered, including a large flint tool 7cm by 2cm described as a polished chisel and dated to about 3000 BC. It was probably intended for use bound to the end of a wood or bone handle and held in place by dried sinew. Similar stone tools of the period have been found elsewhere in the borough at Cheadle and Offerton. At this period farming of animals and crops was first begun and permanent structures for living accommodation were built out of wood, wattle and thatch. A good example of this type of hut which continued into the Iron Age was recreated by the Mellor Archaeological Trust near their excavations with the help of students from Ridge Danyers College.

Bronze Age finds of 2000-1200 BC are even more fruitful in Stockport, although it is safe to say that this area was not one of the most populated at the time. Stone-axe hammers with sharp and blunt ends have been found, as have funeral urns at Portwood, Cheadle and Ludworth Moor – crude baked-clay pots containing the ashes of cremated human remains. There are a number of unexcavated burial mounds – at Werneth Low, Ludworth Moor and probably elsewhere. One, broken open in the nineteenth century, was raided by the peasantry of the neighbourhood, but all they found was a clay pot and an acorn. Another revealed a trench full of red ash and 'spelks of bone'. A farmer called Bagshaw carted away the stone from another on Werneth Low. It is claimed that the bone mill at Turf Lea, Marple, was the recipient of several cartloads of human bones from a mound on Mellor Moor desecrated by a local farmer in the early 1800s.

Despite these depredations by would-be treasure hunters, quite a bit of evidence still remains to tell us something of these ages, for which there is no written record. At the Mellor dig, 140 pieces of 'Mellor Pot' – handmade, undecorated, simple baked clay probably used in cooking – have been recovered. Analysis shows that the clay contains minerals associated with the Bradwell-Castleton area of the Derbyshire Peak District and may be of the late Neolithic-early Bronze Age. By this time a village of huts would have been established on the hill at Mellor, making it the earliest known community in Stockport. Possibly its pots, or the clay for them, was imported from sister communities in the Peak, where larger communities like the one at Mam Tor, the impressive hill fort near Castleton, are known to have existed.

At Bramhall several bronze finds have been made; a barbed and tanged arrowhead alongside flints was found near the Lady Brook. Bronze axe heads known as palstaves have been found in Cheadle Road, Cheadle and between Adswood and Shaw Heath. Other finds were made at Ack Lane and Kitts Moss. Fragments of bronze slag from moulds to make implements or decorative objects have been recovered at Mellor. On nearby Cobden Edge, above Strines Valley, Shaw Cairn was excavated in the 1970s revealing a Bronze-Age burial mound of 2000-900 BC. Situated near the trig point at the highest part of the ridge, with outstanding views over the Cheshire Plain, the mound contained cremated human bones and a decorated earthenware food vessel, perhaps to sustain the deceased in their journey to the other world.

This may indeed have been the edge of the known world for our Mellor hill dwellers, as about 1000-500 BC a deep defensive ditch was constructed around the village to protect it from attack, in a period believed to have been more competitive

Red sandstone bluffs above the Mersey near Lancashire Bridge, 1960s. The rock is very soft and can easily be excavated using simple bone or stone tools to create caves and shelters.

for existing resources. This was the beginning of the warlike Iron Age and traces of iron slag from smelting have been found on the site. Cracked pebbles, which were used to cook food in water-filled pots by being heated and then dropped into the pots, have been excavated in largish quantities. A hammer stone similar to many found in prehistoric copper mines at Alderley Edge, was discovered in a brook on nearby Ludworth Moor, providing a link with the sourcing of copper for bronze manufacture – did a miner drop his axe on a trade visit here?

By AD 79 the Romans had arrived in the North-West and Roman pottery, glassware, tiles, lead discs for use as spindle whorls and coins all cropped up at the Mellor settlement. There are coins of Vespasian AD 69-79, Faustina, wife of Marcus Aurelius, AD 176-180 and Claudius II AD 268-270, but after the end of Roman rule in the fifth century there are no datable finds for 1,000 years, suggesting that the village was abandoned.

There is controversy over whether Stockport ever had a Roman fort or settlement on or near the Market Place. Plenty of evidence exists for Roman roads crossing the borough and Roman finds aplenty back up notions of human activity here, but historians disagree about the fort on 'Castle Yard' overlooking the old ford on the River Mersey. Henry Heginbotham, writing in the 1880s, had no doubts that there was one and cited the discovery of 'tessellated pavement' (tiles) in the castle mound lowered in the 1770s, and a coin of Honorius AD 393-423, as evidence.

It was also claimed that at times of drought when the Mersey ran shallow below the old Castle Hill, near Park Mills where Sainsbury's now stands, an ancient Roman pavement of the old ford could still be seen beneath the water, as recently as the late nineteenth century. Further evidence was uncovered in the digging of foundations at Shawcross Fold, now occupied by Asda, when the alleged remains of a Roman bathhouse were found, suggested by bricks, flooring and roofing tiles.

The nineteenth-century historian Dr Whitaker declared:

> Stockport appears to be a common centre to three or four variously directed ways of the Romans ... these are sure signatures of a station here. It was therefore fixed on the plane of the Castle Hill ... that is exactly such a position as the Romans would instantly select for the station ... it is a square knoll which looks down upon a rocky bank and is guarded by the Mersey at the foot of it.

He was supported in these assertions by subsequent historians the Revd John Watson, the Revd William Marriott and Dr Ormerod, among others.

Even later evidence has failed to convince modern historians of the presence of a substantial Roman fort at Stockport. A tile stamped 'LM' and resembling Roman coarseware was uncovered during the digging of a police parade room at the rear of the old Courthouse on Vernon Street, which backed onto Castle Yard, in the late nineteenth century. A coin of Gallienus AD 253-268 was found in the sand of the Mersey nearby and a hoard of Roman coins of AD 375-378 were again found near the Mersey when Daw Bank bus station was built in the 1970s. Dr Peter Arrowsmith, writing in 1997, described the catalogue of known

Above left: According to local legend Druids are supposed to have incited the local population to war by sacrificing a maiden on Ludworth Moor in order to gain victory in battle.

Above right: These stones on Ludworth Moor are traditionally linked to the Druids and early inhabitants of the area. A Bronze Age burial mound is in the wood on the horizon, above Marple Bridge.

Roman finds in Stockport as slim, but observed that some form of site probably existed here, centred on Castle Hill, though its nature remained elusive.

At the time of the Roman takeover, it is said that this part of Britain was occupied by two confederations of tribes – the Brigantes of Lancashire and Yorkshire, and the Cornavii of Cheshire and Derbyshire – with what is now the Mersey river as a fluctuating boundary between them. The Romans named this region, bounded by the Mersey, Flavia Caesariensis, which was first occupied by the legion belonging to Agricola, Governor of Britannia, who visited Manchester (then named Mancenium) in AD 79 and ordered its defences, which can still be seen today at Castlefield.

Quite probably he visited Stockport, which was a crossing point for several Roman roads and may have had a fort, but he is unlikely to have spared it more than a passing glance. The Romans and Romano-British Celtic peoples continued to rub shoulders for the next 300-400 years. Roman coins dating from the first to the fourth century have been found all over the present borough, as have other artefacts including pottery shards, a quern stone for grinding corn by hand, and even a gaming counter. It is likely that settlements existed at Bramhall Green, Cheadle, Mile End and Romiley, where prevalent finds indicate human activity. Since the advent of metal detectors, the amount of metalware from the period has increased dramatically and much remains in private collections. One silver coin was even turned up by a postman doing his rounds when he saw it glinting in roadwork diggings at Mile End.

The most probable Roman road to cross the borough travelled from Manchester to Buxton, then as now an inland spa town. Heading down Lancashire Hill along Old Road, it crossed the Mersey by a paved ford below the Roman fortlet on Castle Hill, just about where the new 'Courts' shopping precinct now stands. Once legionnaires may have stared down at a crystal stream running through a red sandstone gorge, filled with sea trout and salmon in season, and watched the eight-wheeled oxcarts, the delivery vehicles of the empire, splashing through the shallow ford below this hill.

Southward through Offerton and on past Broadoak Moat at Torkington, over Jacksons Edge Road at High Lane and through Disley, via Buxton Old Road, this ancient route heads into the Derbyshire Hills. It is said that in a lonely wind gap above Whaley Bridge, Romans carved graffiti on rocks in Latin about their sexual exploits with slave girls – old, but still legible.

Another road on an east/west axis may have crossed the borough from Cheadle through Stockport and Bredbury heading for the fort at Melandra near Glossop. A section of this road was uncovered at Cheadle Heath in the nineteenth century, according to the historian Fletcher Moss. Its western end linked to the main Chester to Manchester route. This road may have crossed Werneth Low, where a Roman signal station and a Romano-British farmhouse are known to have existed, on the fringe of the Pennine hills. The place name Werneth is said to derive from the Celtic 'gwern', the alder tree which still grows abundantly in the boggy valleys nearby. In Bredbury, two field names with Roman connotations exist at Street Acre and Pavement Head. Apple Street is a continuation of this route on the Glossop side of Werneth Low.

A further Roman road may have headed through Cheadle from Manchester and on to Bramhall via Ack Lane East towards the hills and Pott Shrigley. It could have linked settlements along the route at Cheadle, Bramhall and elsewhere, eventually reaching Buxton. It is interesting that Celtic place names at Mellor (bare hill), Werneth (alders) and Cheadle (a wood) coincide with places having Romano-British finds.

By the fifth century the 'Victorious' 20th Legion, long stationed in Cheshire, was recalled to defend the Empire and the region we now call Stockport was left to the depredations of incomers like the Picts and Scots, not renowned for their peace-loving qualities. Their efforts were soon supplemented by those of the Anglo-Saxons and Jutes from Northern Germany and Jutland. These had been invited over to help get rid of the Picts but soon decided that land-grabbing was their special talent, so the too-civilised Romano-Britons were either decimated, driven westwards, or compromised with their new neighbours.

In the North of what rapidly became England it was the Angles who settled in largely tribal groups and they left their old English place names all over

Above left: Roman coins have been found around the borough – these are from Cheadle and Heald Green.

Above right: A Romano-British quern stone found near a Roman road in Bramhall, used for grinding corn by hand.

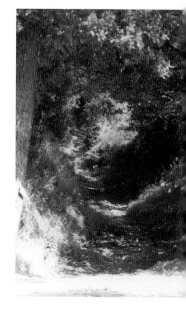

This tree-lined overgrown track washes down large pebbles after every heavy rain. Deeply scoured now, it may be the remains of a Roman road crossing Werneth Low near Compstall, dating to AD 80.

14

Stockport. These people are interesting to us because they were our ancestral forefathers and the founders of what became one of the most important towns in Cheshire.

But beginnings were modest. The earliest datable place names of the period are Bosden in Hazel Grove, meaning 'Bosa's hill', which would have been a settlement from at least the seventh century, Bredbury, the 'burh built of planks', and Norbury, again with the burh element implying a fortified place of some importance. Interestingly, at each of these places coal seams crop the surface; were Anglo-Saxons the earliest exploiters of the black stuff? The rivers Tame and Mersey seem again to have formed a boundary between two Anglian kingdoms – those of Mercia south of the Mersey and Northumbria on the Lancashire and Yorkshire side to the north. Mersey is Old English for 'river at the boundary' although Tame is of British origin, showing mothers were still teaching their children Celtic words even though their fathers may have been Anglo-Saxon.

Chance finds of Anglo-Saxon date in the borough include six silver coins of King Eadred AD 946-55 and Edmund AD 939-46 found at Reddish Green in 1789, and fragments of Anglian crosses at Cheadle, one of which is exhibited inside the parish church. It is said that an older cross with a rounded shaft of a type known as 'Mercian', often used as a boundary marker, was dug up in a field near Cheadle church.

The name Stockport has led to speculation, earlier historians confidently declaring it to mean 'a stockaded place in a wood' though now the earliest recorded spelling of twelfth-century date is said to signify stoke 'a settlement' and port 'a market place'. Later versions have appeared on maps including Stopford, Stopwash and Stopport. It is interesting to note that modern inhabitants usually pronounce the name as 'Stopport'. Did 'Stokeport' have a market in Anglo-Saxon times? Given its position at the intersection of important route ways and the possibility of a fort here, the likelihood of a market is very strong. It certainly existed by the twelfth century when the Norman castle was built.

Bredbury is an Anglo-Saxon name meaning 'burh built of planks' and Goyt Hall, Lower Bredbury, is one of the oldest houses in the area, pictured here in 1880.

ANGLIAN CROSS
CIRCA 11TH CENTURY
FOUND NEAR THE
PARISH CHURCH, CHEADLE,
IN 1874.

The Danish and Viking invasions began to disrupt the Anglo-Saxon kingdoms from AD 835 and by the 900s Cheshire was subject to depredations from the North. A granddaughter of King Alfred, Princess Ethelfleada, became famous for leading her Mercian troops to battle against both the Danes and the Welsh. She was the wife of the Earl of Mercia, by this time a sub-kingdom of Wessex, and her brother King Edward the Elder established a series of forts along the Mersey Valley facing threats from Viking-controlled Northumbria. Ethelfleada led most of the fighting, driving the heathen Vikings back in a series of raids as far north as York. It is tempting to think of her as a possible founder of the Anglo-Saxon fortress and town of Stokeport in the years AD 910-918. At this time Cheadle was probably a more important settlement than Stokeport and the Anglo-Saxon crosses found there may testify to this fact.

There is a local tradition of a defeat of Vikings at Stockport by local warriors in this period. Writing in the eighteenth century, local historian John Watson ascribed the finding of numerous human bones beside the Mersey, during the construction of Park Mills, to this sanguinary engagement. As recently as the 1980s further human bones were said to have been uncovered during the digging of Sainsbury's underground car park on the same spot. Numerous other bones have been recovered in and around the castle mound nearby, where the 'Courts' development now stands. Was some attempt made on an Anglo-Saxon fort here and repulsed with heavy loss? The legend of Nico ditch, an earthwork which passes through Reddish, supports the notion of a desperate fight between Saxons and Danes hereabouts. The ditch was supposedly dug in one night to defend Manchester against the Danes and the battle gave Reddish (Red ditch) and Gorton (Gore town) their subsequent names.

Little in the way of Scandinavian place-name evidence suggests scanty settlement locally by Danes or Vikings. The southern side of the Mersey seems to have remained resolutely Anglo-Saxon, particularly after the great Battle of

Above left: Shuttleworth's painting of Stockport market in the 1800s. Was there a market here from Saxon times?

Above right: A fragmented 'Anglian'-style cross found 300 yards from the present church in Cheadle, thought to date from the eleventh century.

Above: Princess Ethelfleada, Saxon princess and granddaughter of King Alfred, may have been the founder of Stokeport. She led her troops into battle, driving back the Welsh and the Danes and built forts along the Mersey.

Right: This photograph taken in 1965 shows old stone steps to the Mersey beside the Buck and Dog and across the river the traditional site of a battle between Saxons and Danes. When Park Mills was built large quantities of human bones were found there.

Brunanburh fought near the Mersey estuary at Bromborough utterly defeated the Viking threat in AD 937, when an army under King Athelstane killed five kings and seven earls who had arrived in a great fleet of 615 ships. 'Never before in all this island, as ancient sages say, was an army put to greater slaughter', recorded the *Anglo-Saxon Chronicle*.

The few local names of Danish origin – 'hulme' as in Cheadle Hulme, 'kirk' as in Chadkirk, Romiley, and gate or 'gata' meaning street, as in Hillgate, Churchgate, Chestergate, are said to have been later influences after the Viking threat had subsided.

Chapter 2

Medieval Manor

The last great challenge from Nordic invaders came in 1066. Stokeport had seen armies of Danes from Northumbria and Norse from Ireland and the Western Isles, now a fleet from Norway landed in Yorkshire but was quickly defeated, followed immediately by the defeat of the Anglo-Saxon royal army by Norman invaders.

In Cheshire these events seemed far away and defiance of Norman edicts led to a terrible destruction in the North. William, Duke of Normandy, now King of England, led an army against 'his own people'. He devastated the North-East, killing people and animals, burning towns and villages and making bonfires of farming implements and food stores. In the winter of 1069-70 he crossed the Pennines and attacked Cheshire, defeating a combined army of English and Welsh who had garrisoned Chester. A ferocious warlord, Hugh Lupus (the Wolf), was set to govern by the sword as the first Norman Earl of Chester. Cheshire was wasted and most of the Anglo-Saxon lords were evicted. Lupus appointed warlike Norman barons to serve under him and gave them the vacant manors.

The Domesday survey carried out in 1086 revealed the destruction. Bramale (Bramhall) had fallen from thirty-two shillings in 1066 to just five shillings in value. Nordberie (Norbury) fell from ten shillings to three shillings and local lords Brun and Hacon had been replaced by swaggering Normans Hamo de Massey at Bramhall and Bigot de Losges at Norbury. Werneth, Romiley and Leighton in Marple had suffered similar fates. Their collective value was reduced to a quarter, and the Domesday chronicler adds the sinister note that, on acquisition, the Norman lord 'found it waste'.

Two notable local exceptions to this rule were the manors of Cedde (Cheadle, or possibly Chadkirk) and Bretberie (Bredbury) both still retaining their 1066 value of ten shillings each and still held by their Anglo-Saxon thanes. Gamel held Cheadle under the Earl of Chester and Wulfric held Bredbury for Richard de Vernon, a wealthy Cheshire baron. Why this was so we can only speculate, but it has been suggested that Wulfric may have acted as a steward of north-east Cheshire and his local knowledge would have been useful to the Norman

Above left: Hugh Lupus'
sword, carried as State Sword
at coronations, conferred the
earl's power over Cheshire
direct from the king 'to hold as
freely by the sword as the king
held England by his crown'.

Above right: The castle of
Stokeport as visualised by
Henry Heginbotham in 1880,
based on the sketch plan
of the foundations made by
John Watson in 1775 and
Heginbotham's assumption
that Stokeport would have
resembled Halton Castle,
above the Mersey in Cheshire.

overlords. He also held the manor of Offerton, which was valued at five shillings and, curiously, had been waste before 1066.

At the time of the Domesday survey, Stokeport itself was probably a minor settlement with a role as a trading place in a position central to surrounding communities. It is not mentioned at all in the Domesday survey – but then neither was London! The first written reference to Stockport as a place was in 1173, in the following century, when it was important enough to have a castle. We know this because in that year it was held in a revolt against the king, Henry II, by Geoffrey de Costentin, a partisan of the Earl of Chester, who had joined with Henry's sons to defy the king's royal authority. This was a mistake for Costentin because it cost him his manor of Stockport and other estates in Staffordshire and Ireland confiscated by the king. It is likely that the castle at Stockport was first built during the civil wars of King Stephen and the Empress Matilda in the troublesome times of the 1150s and would have been a mere earthen mound with a wooden palisade and tower on the site of the rock above the ford which now, considerably lowered, is Castle Yard.

Many such castles were erected at this lawless time and robber barons inflicted untold tortures and miseries on anyone from whom they could extort wealth. The people were so afraid of their Norman overlords that it is said a considerable body of them would take flight at the sight of just three or four horsemen.

Following Geoffrey de Costentin, the next recorded lord of Stockport was Robert de Stokeport in the 1180s, who was probably, according to historian Dr Peter Arrowsmith, the son of Waltheof, himself the son of Wulfric the Anglo-Saxon thane. Robert was the first of three Robert de Stokeports, and though English, the Normanised style of their names reflected the use of Norman French among all the land-holding classes and anyone with recourse to legal documents.

A gabled building opposite St Mary's church on Rostron Brow was thought to be the first priest's house and may have been occupied since Matthew 'Clericus', *c.* 1190. It would have been rebuilt over the years and shows a Tudor style in this engraving of 1880.

It is also believed that Stockport was the head manor of a collection of lesser manors constituting a barony, which was possibly why a castle was built. Hugh Lupus, the first Earl of Chester, had created eight baronies, but Stockport does not seem to have been among these. It was a later creation and contained manors not held directly from the earl but from lesser lords like Hamo de Massey (Bredbury and Brinnington). It was certainly in existence by the 1180-90s and it was then that we first hear of 'Matthew', clerk of Stockport, witnessing a charter granted to Robert de Stokeport I. This Matthew is claimed as the first priest and it is surmised a simple wooden chapel may have existed at this time. However, the first definite reference to a 'parson of Stockport' is that of Robert de Worth in the 1200s and older parts of the present parish church, notably the vestry and chantry, are reputed to date to the thirteenth century.

It is quite likely that a market continued to be held at Stockport throughout this period but by 1260 it was formally ratified through a charter granted to local lord Robert de Stokeport III by Prince Edward, Earl of Chester. In turn Robert was able to charge tolls (a tax on produce) and stallage (rent for the stalls), thus making his lordship more profitable and paying a fee to the earl for this privilege. The charter allowed a market to be held every Thursday (later Friday) and a fair on St Wilfrid's Day for eight days following (from 12 October) annually.

By this time Stockport would have consisted of the wooden staved and palisaded castle, a small chapel at the other end of the Market Place on a hill above the Underbanks, and low, single-storey, timber-framed and thatched dwellings, clustered between, issuing smoke from smoke holes or louvres in their simple roofs. Fires had to be extinguished between the hours of 8 p.m.

and 8 a.m. and a curfew bell was rung for this purpose until as late as the nineteenth century.

By the 1300s the parish church seems to have been rebuilt in local red sandstone, probably during the rectorship of Richard de Vernon, priest at Stockport from 1306 to 1334. His life-sized effigy in similar red stone lies in the Easter sepulchre near the altar –still housed within the old stone chancel he is believed to have built. He was a son of the wealthy Baron of Shipbrooke in Cheshire and may have been able to provide funds for the project. Also, the rebuilding may have coincided with a transformation of the castle at the other end of the Market Place which was replaced by a ringwork of stone walling around the Castle Hill and possibly town revetment walls encircling the Market Place itself.

The quarry for this stone is most likely to have been the Castle Hill itself. A stone-arched bridge over the Mersey, below the castle and downstream from the ford, was also erected at about this time. Work on the old Castle Hill in 2003-04 still revealed vast amounts of bunter sandstone, fifty lorry loads a day being excavated to make way for the new Courts shopping development. Also revealed was the remains of the castle well, clearly showing the old handpick marks made by the men who cut it, and containing shards of glazed medieval pottery, animal bones and ancient cobblestones. At the time of writing (2004) these have yet to be dated.

The bridge over the Mersey is said to have been built by the 1280s and had a small chapel or hermitage at one end where masses were said for travellers by a priest known as 'the hermit of Stokeport' who was licensed by the Bishop of Lichfield on an annual or bi-annual basis. These priests were not so poor, having

Below left: During excavations on the site of the old castle in 2003, a medieval well containing pottery fragments, bones and cobblestones was discovered, clearly showing the pickmarks of the original excavators.

Below right: The Mersey was always an obstacle for travellers and this view shows how a later age bridged the gap with the railway viaduct and road bridge.

land and rents dedicated to their use, and the office of hermit was sought after, being occupied by several people in a short space of time. The bridge definitely helped the development of the market, being the first across the Mersey at that time, but it may also have had a military purpose.

Lancashire Bridge, as we call it, lay below the old castle and if the stone to build it came from the Castle Hill, then much higher than it is now, its building may have coincided with the strengthening of the castle itself. The 1280s were a time of military activity in Cheshire when Stockport bowyers and arrowsmiths were busy making arms for the supply of King Edward I's invading army and the garrisons of his castles in Wales. The bridge at Stockport was effectively the hinge of a door which opened into Wales from the North of England – ideal for the movement of large amounts of men and equipment, and a vital communication route to Scotland, Edward's next objective.

Elaborate features in Richard de Vernon's new chancel included carved seats for the clergy, a double piscina to hold water for celebrating mass, a high cruck-beamed roof and delicate stonework tracery in the windows.

By the time Richard de Vernon was Rector of Stockport, Edward was dead and his son, Edward II, was a notably weak king. Scottish raids across the border came as far south as Skipton, within fifty miles of Stockport. Over eighty towns and villages were burned in the North and grants were provided for towns to strengthen their defences. Were Stockport's 'town walls' erected at this time? Sections still exist behind and above the Underbanks around the Market Place, despite the encroachments of latter years. Stockport manor was held at this time by the lords of Stockport from the de Spenser feudal estates. This family were favourites of Edward II, so any cash grants would probably have been available to them for use in preserving their estates ahead of anyone else.

As late as 1775 a series of angular walls crowned Castle Hill, sketched by local historian John Watson, and appearing on a manorial estate plan of the period. In the previous century they had been represented as a ring of walls on the 1680 map of Stockport.

The medieval barony stretched from Bredbury and Brinnington in the north to Poynton and Woodford in the south. Cheadle and Bramhall were held by other

Sections of the old town wall photographed in the nineteenth century and bearing a strong resemblance to the red sandstone walls of Chester.

An eighteenth-century view of Stockport centre including the church, castle mill, old corn mill and meadows, so close to the town.

lords, as were Heaton Norris and Reddish. The de Stokeports died out in 1292, when the barony passed through the de Etons to the Warrens, who were lords of the manor until the death of Sir George Warren in 1801.

One of the outstanding products of the area in medieval times were the Cheshire archers, largely recruited from the Macclesfield Hundred, which included Stockport, who provided the royal bodyguard for Richard II and distinguished themselves in the wars in France under Edward III and his warlike son, the Black Prince.

The twelfth-century hunting forest of Ullerswood, owned by the barons of Dunham Massey, encroached on part of Stockport at Heald Green, so when the de Masseys granted the barony of Stockport to their vassal, Robert de Stokeport, they reserved their right to hunt game.

The much larger royal forests of the Peak and Macclesfield also covered parts of the borough. Macclesfield Forest had belonged to the Norman earls of Chester but, on the death of the last, reverted to the king's eldest son, who became traditionally Prince of Wales and Earl of Chester. Several local families held office as foresters including the Davenports of Bramall Hall, the Leghs of Adlington and the Vernons of Marple. In the Peak Forest a local family, the de Meleurs of Mellor, who lived at Mellor Hall, enforced the harsh forest laws around Ludworth.

Macclesfield Forest included parts of modern Stockport – all of Marple and parts of Bosden, Torkington and Norbury, in present-day Hazel Grove. Its centre was Macclesfield itself and here the Prince of Wales had a hunting lodge. This forest was frequently hunted by the Black Prince, son of Edward III and victor

Above: A Cheshire archer at the Battle
Crecy in France – many such men were
recruited in the Hundred of Macclesfield
included Stokeport.

Left above: The Davenport of Bramhall
was a felon's head (busts by fireplace),
here displayed in the Great Hall at Bram
– symbol of their rights as hereditary for
to execute malefactors.

Left below: Bramall Hall was on the edg
the Forest of Macclesfield. Arrowheads
been found embedded deep inside the
of ancient trees on the estate. One suc
exhibited at the hall.

of the Battles of Crecy and Poitiers in France. These battles were largely won
by the English longbowmen and the prince had instructed his officials to take
'only the best' from the Hundred of Macclesfield, where he had been impressed
by the skill of local huntsmen and archers. From this time a hundred Cheshire
bowmen traditionally formed the royal bodyguard.

Clearance of parts of the forests was sometimes a reward for military service
to the Crown. Captain of the archers, William Jodrell, was given leave to take
oak from the forest of Macclesfield to repair his house. Sir Thomas Danyers
was given land at Lyme near Disley to create a hunting park and lodge – now
Lyme Hall and Park. Richard de Vernon, Lord of Marple, reclaimed land around
Torkington Brook as early as the 1220s. In the 1250s the Abbot of Basingwerk
had ordered the systematic felling of trees around Ludworth, part of the manor
of Glossop, which had been given to the abbey. However, any alterations to the
forest had to consider the deer and if the royal rights of 'venison' were infringed
it was an offence punishable by fines for the rich and worse for the poor.

Above: Marple church on the Ridge was built by Samuel Oldknow many years after Marple had ceased to be a part of the Forest of Macclesfield.

Right above: The house at Broadoak, Torkington, was built in the forest by John de Legh, who created a wide moat to keep his many enemies at bay, in about 1354.

Right below: The moated Arden Hall still has a bridge over what is now the dry moat of the house at Bredbury. Victorian schoolchildren remembered being charged sixpence to go up the repaired tower to admire the local views.

A house with a moat at Broadoak, Torkington was built by John de Legh on sixty acres of cleared woodland in 1354. It was within the Forest of Macclesfield and is said to have had two chambers and a kitchen with a barn, stables and fields nearby. John de Legh was a follower of the Duke of Lancaster and a ruffian who didn't stop at theft and murder to advance his career, 'activities common to other landowners in the region during this period', according to Dr Arrowsmith.

Sir John Hyde of Hyde and Norbury was the leader of a band of seventy-one archers under the Black Prince in France and fought at Crecy and Poitiers. He was violent and corrupt; being found guilty in 1353 of mutilating a servant, he also took bribes from men wishing to avoid recruitment as archers in the Black Prince's army. A dispute with his neighbours, the de Hondefords, resulted in Hyde's murder of Geoffrey de Hondeford in 1360, for which he received a royal pardon.

Two other moated halls existed: at Reddish Hall, on the present golf course by Vale Road, and at Arden Hall, Bredbury, where the remains of the moat are now

Far left: A rider is crudely carved on the stone font at Mellor, believed to date to Saxon or Norman times.

Left: Lovely medieval carving on the ancient oak pulpit at Mellor church dates to the fourteenth century and may be the oldest in England.

dry. Reddish Hall was an intricate timber-framed structure since demolished, but Arden Hall remains, incorporating some older timber work in its sixteenth-century present stone structure. The turbulent days of the fourteenth century are given as the reason for the construction of moated sites, when land-grabbers and landholders defended their territories against each other at a time when central authority was weakened.

Another moated site is Peel Moat, again on a golf course, this time in Heaton Moor. It is quite small, but is possibly the remains of the manor house of Heaton Norris, which once included Heaton Moor, recorded in 1282. The moat is still waterlogged and bricks and stones from an old building have been found.

Two other early medieval artefacts in the borough which deserve a mention are the font and pulpit at Mellor church. A chapel of ease for the parish of Glossop, built within the most ancient habitation of Mellor hillfort, it contains a crude stone font carved with a simplistic figure of a horse and rider and may date from Norman times. The pulpit, carved from a single oak log, shows the early English Gothic style of the fourteenth century and could be the oldest wooden pulpit in England. It was once ordered to be chopped up by a 'modernising' vicar but happily defied the woodsman's axe and was allowed to remain.

Chapter 3

Staircase House and Market Place

The first borough charter seems to have been granted by 1220 but this was ratified by the charter of 1260 when Prince Edward, Earl of Chester, gave Robert de Stokeport rights to hold a market weekly and a fair annually on St Wilfrid's Day. This sealed the commercial success of Stockport, which now rivalled the markets of Macclesfield and Salford, both within the ten-mile radius from which Stockport drew both its custom and its traders – many would have to drive livestock to and from the market, an activity which seldom exceeded a round trip of twenty miles in a day.

The borough charter also gave important rights to the free traders, or burgesses, who lived and worked within the borough. In return for a rental of one shilling annually to the lord of Stockport, they each received a perch of land to build a house, usually around the Market Place or Underbanks on a long narrow strip of land termed a 'burgage' plot. They could take the timber needed from the lord's woods, graze cattle on the common pasture, feed their pigs in the woodlands and take peat for burning as fuel from the bogs or mosslands which then surrounded the town. Great Moor and Little Moor are reminders of such locations, once ill-drained and uninhabited, but now pleasant suburbs.

The burgesses were also exempt from paying toll and stallage both in Stockport and at all the markets and fairs of Cheshire with the exception of the toll on salt from the 'wiches' where the salt mines were. In return, they were expected to grind their corn at the lord's mill, from which he took a proportion, and bake their bread at his manorial bread ovens. If they sold, leased or bequeathed their burgages they paid a fee to the lord for the privilege. There were probably only sixty burgesses in 1260 but by 1483 they had increased to ninety-three, many of whom were wealthy gentry or merchants who leased out their plots to tenants for rental. In that year, for example, Robert Legh, Lord of Adlington, owned ten

Stockport market was thriving from the time of the borough charter in 1220. This is a 1907 postcard view.

A view up Millgate in the early nineteenth century showing an old thatched cottage of medieval date. Millgate led to a manorial corn mill on the Goyt where burgesses ground their corn.

burgages, John Arderne of Bredbury held eight and the Duckenfield family, Lords of Brinnington, held five.

Trades in medieval Stockport are known to have included weaving cloth, baking bread and brewing while Roger le Bower and John le Smith supplied forty-two bows and twenty-four lance heads respectively for the Black Prince's castles at Chester, Flint and Rhuddlan. The Dodge family became wealthy merchants and in 1478 'Oliver Dogge, of Stockport' is recorded as buying three packs of woollen cloth worth £40 in Chester and hiring a ship to carry them to Ireland. In 1483 the Dodges held six burgages in the town, and centuries later their descendants founded Dodge City in America.

The borough was governed by baronial courts, the records of which date back to the thirteenth century. As late as 1833 John Kenyon Winterbottom, steward of the Court Baron, gave evidence that a consecutive series of these rolls existed for the previous 300 years, with a few from earlier centuries. The court leet was empowered to hear and punish all crimes in the neighbourhood. It developed from the portmoot which was composed of burgesses, the chief of whom came

Top left: Medieval sandstone walling discovered in the old court leet building during renovations in 1999 had been covered with panelling.

Top right: The stocks were re-introduced to Stockport by the Heritage Trust, unfortunately only nice people are allowed in them!

Above left: A small hatch led into one arched cell below the road level.

Above right: The dungeon and courthouse were at the top of Mealhouse – or Dungeon Brow – leading onto the Market Place.

to be known as mayor; the first recorded is William de Baggilegh in 1296. The courts appointed all officers of the town, including two constables elected on a yearly basis, market overlookers, bailiffs and so on.

It was stated in an ancient document that, 'the mayor governs the town as the chief officer, punishing all offenders against the peace with the dungeon, the stocks, and the ducking stool'. A number of traditional punishments were kept up until the mid-eighteenth century. One of these was the brank, an iron-looped hood with a spiked tongue piece, designed to dissuade scolding women when all else failed. Stockport's brank – or scold's bridle – was said to be one of the most vicious in Cheshire. The ducking stool was usually a chair attached to a long pole in which the offender was swung out over a pond and ducked 'as often as the case required'. This punishment dated back to the Anglo-Saxons and in Stockport two ducking sites existed – one at Daw Bank near the present bus station and another at Cale Green.

The stocks were situated near the church gates on the Market Place, but the unruly language of the detainees, secured by their legs for disorderly

behaviour, offended churchgoers and they were removed closer to the dungeon on Mealhouse Brow. The dungeon itself consisted of a number of chambers, some hewn out of solid rock and one at a considerable depth down the Brow. Generally small with an arched roof, they were quite soundproof and must have been a good place in which to sober up quickly.

More severe punishments included flogging, which was carried out with the offender tied to a T-shaped whipping post erected in the middle of the Market Place. Sometimes the post was placed on a cart and conveyed to a place more convenient for the large crowds of onlookers. A whip with nine lashes was used and the culprits, frequently petty offenders, were stripped to the waist to receive the prescribed number of strokes. Constables' accounts show that this punishment was still in use as late as 1820. Whipping was often handed out as a deterrent to vagrants and was applied for as minor a crime as stealing a handkerchief, often accompanied by imprisonment.

The next most serious punishment was the pillory – a small platform on which the offender stood with head and hands secured in a wooden frame. It was used on the Market Place and the mob of onlookers were free to pelt the unfortunate victim with any foul object that came to hand – dead cats, rotten eggs and old vegetables. Sometimes serious injury ensued and the loss of an eye was not uncommon. Dr Heginbotham, writing in 1882, stated that it had not then been used for fifty years.

In medieval times, however, more extreme penalties were applied locally. The forest laws required that poachers be executed or blinded and this right to dispense justice was vested in hereditary 'sergeants of the forest' like the Davenports of Bramhall, whose family crest depicts a felon with a rope around his throat, known locally as 'the thief's neck'. This is the popular name of a public house in Woodford, otherwise known as the Davenport Arms.

The Warrens, who became the Lords of Stockport, also claimed the right of 'infangthief' – that is to execute justice upon thieves – and the mayors of Stockport

Above left: A whipping post was erected in the middle of the market but had been discontinued by the time of this picture in 1850. It was kept until the twentieth century at the top of High Bankside.

Above right: The brank or scold's bridle was a vicious implement intended for the control of nagging and foul-mouthed women.

may well have referred miscreants to the Lord of the Manor for more severe penalties to be carried into effect. In those days justice was seen to be done.

Following the death of the last de Stokeport lord in 1292, the barony passed through marriage to the de Etons, whose double-headed eagle came to be incorporated in the Stockport heraldic coat of arms. In the late fourteenth century the Warrens inherited and remained Lords of Stockport until the death of Sir George Warren in 1801. His medieval predecessor, Sir John Warren, was in 1490 challenged on his right of infangthief by Prince Arthur, Earl of Chester and son of Henry VII. He replied in his defence that a thief taken in his manor of Stockport, found guilty and sentenced to death should be brought 'to his own proper gallows and there hanged'. He also claimed right of 'outfangthief' whereby tenants of his, found guilty of offences elsewhere, should be brought and hanged on his gallows 'by servants of the said John'. Keeping justice in-house must have been good for morale.

Scottish raids into Northern England continued to worry the inhabitants of Stockport until the 1330s and it is very probable that the curtain wall around the Castle Hill and Market Place was constructed at this time. A series of cells seem to have been made in the building later known as the court leet or mealhouse (it had a double function). These have been uncovered in recent building renovations. One has an arched medieval doorway, now blocked with eighteenth-century bricks, through what was the town wall. Another, lower down Mealhouse Brow, also accessed via the medieval town wall, is carved from solid rock, its barrel-vaulted roof lined with brick in the eighteenth century.

The troubled century continued, with archers departing for the Hundred Years' War with France, the onset of a decimating plague, the Black Death, and the Peasants' Revolt, which shook the nobility and undermined the feudal system. Merchant classes and freemen, who formed themselves into powerful trade guilds, were gaining wealth and influence. Then the lords began to fight among themselves and the crown itself was contested for in an unruly scramble for power.

When the first timbers that were to form the upright cruck frames of Staircase House were cut in the winter of 1459, the nobles of England had been hacking

A sixteenth-century view of the old Market Hall in Stockport by artist David Kelsall.

at one another with bands of armed retainers for almost a decade. In that same year Cheshire men were slaughtered fighting on both sides in the Battle of Blore Heath where 2,400 perished with Lord Audley, their leader, who was marching to the assistance of the king's forces. Soon after, the greatest battle ever recorded on English soil drenched the fields of Towton with English blood, just over fifty miles from Stockport. It was a battle fought between archers, and the 40,000 casualties may have included local men.

But business went on as usual – the Wars of the Roses of Lancaster and York did not disrupt trade. The great commercial centres thrived, despite the loss of English provinces in France. On a modest scale this was represented by the building and growth of a merchant's warehouse, workshop and home, fronting the Market Place in Stockport, which we now call Staircase House. Various trades were carried on there – cheese factoring, wine importation, soap and tallow manufacturing all took a turn. From a simple rectangular building, open to the rafters and not unlike a barn, the house grew and prospered, being extended down the hill at the rear with courtyards and extra wings. The freemen of Stockport were exercising their right to become rich.

One such was Edmond Shaa or Shaw, son of a mercer from Dukinfield, which was then in Stockport parish. Edmond Shaa became a London goldsmith, a royal jeweller and master of the King's Mint. As Lord Mayor of London at the coronation of Richard III, he presented the wine cup, a high honour, but one nearly followed by disaster as his royal patron was defeated and killed at the Battle of Bosworth two years later in 1485. He retained the patronage of the next king, Henry VII, because of his great wealth and influence.

Edmond died soon after and his will of 1487 left a handsome bequest to his native town, founding a grammar school in Stockport, only the third such free 'public school' in the country after Winchester and Eton. A priest was also employed to pray for his soul and those of his mother and father at both Stockport and in a chantry chapel he founded in the pass over the Pennines into Yorkshire at Woodhead. The earliest school is thought to have been

Staircase House as it appeared in about 1800, refronted in brick which concealed the medieval cruck frames.

conducted in an upper room over the vestry in the parish church on Stockport Market Place. Later it occupied a building on Chestergate. The Goldsmiths Company administered a bequest of property owned by Shaa in London to pay for the running of the school.

Vestiges of this increasingly modern age of trade can be found in the buildings which reflect the growth of wealth in the more stable period of the Tudor dynasty. The charming rustic red sandstone St Mary's church in Cheadle dates from 1520-56. It is a fine example of Tudor workmanship and once bore the Royal Arms of Tudor and shields of the three leading local gentry families of Bulkeley, Savage and Brereton who helped fund the edifice.

In 1513 local men fought in the Battle of Flodden against the Scots, with many archers recruited in Cheshire and Lancashire. Two leaders were Sir John Stanley and William Honford of Handforth Hall, who was killed in the battle. Sir John returned and married Margaret Honford, the daughter of his comrade-in-arms. He built a chantry chapel in both Manchester Cathedral and at Cheadle church in 1525, with an inscription in stained glass. It is thought that the effigies of the two knights in armour, side by side, at Cheadle may be those of Sir John

This building was once the rector's own courthouse adjoining his medieval house, but then became a pub, the Pack Horse, with a new frontage further from the roadway.

A busy scene on Little Underbank near the old Albion Hotel and Mealhouse Brow, reflecting the trading prosperity of Stockport town centre in 1910.

The old chancel at St Mary's, Stockport was the burial place of many leading gentry and clergy of the town.

Armoured stone effigies of knightly Honfords, Bulkeleys and Breretons, lords of Handforth and Cheadle, rest in St Mary's parish church, Cheadle.

and William Honford, but could be of an even earlier period, possibly Honfords or Bulkeleys, about 1450, from a previous church on the site.

Sir John Stanley's marriage to Lady Margaret did not endure. He married her when she was just twelve years old, but in 1528 they mutually consented to a divorce and he became a monk in Westminster Abbey, eventually dying there. He was a natural son of James Stanley, Bishop of Ely, a former Warden of Manchester Collegiate church (later the cathedral), so perhaps had a leaning to an ecclesiastical life. Others state he was disappointed in legal disputes over land, or had witnessed traumatic scenes of depredation on campaign in Scotland and became disillusioned with the world. Many local men never returned from the Battle of Flodden and losses meant the Town Council of Macclesfield could not make a quorum to hold their meetings. Lady Margaret married Sir Urian Brereton in 1530 and her descendants are buried in the chapel Stanley had built to commemorate himself and her father. Such are the vagaries of vanity and fortune.

Chapter 4

Civil War: Colonel Duckenfield and the Battle of Stockport

When the ruption occurred which led to civil war between King Charles I and Parliament in 1642, no one in Stockport had any idea what was about to happen. Like many other towns and villages in Cheshire they eagerly subscribed their names to a petition urging neutrality in the county, 'to spare us the horrors of Civil War'. Those who signed the Cheshire Remonstrance included 159 from Stockport, ninety-four from Marple and thirty-eight from Bredbury, but many of these men later became combatants in the war, perhaps reluctantly.

Events moved quickly and in September local Royalist magnate, Lord Strange, menaced the town of Manchester which had refused to give up the arms and gunpowder he demanded for the king's army. The town was fortified and a call went out to supporters of Parliament to help defend the place from his lordship, who was bringing a small army of his own to lay siege until he got his gunpowder. Among local gentry and their tenants who responded to the call to defend parliamentary rights and liberty were Robert Duckenfield, a youth in his early twenties, but already lord of the manors of Dukinfield and Portwood; his neighbour, Ralph Arderne of Arden Hall, Bredbury, Edward Hyde of Norbury and his relations the Hydes of Denton, the Hollands of Denton Hall, Henry Bradshawe of Marple and Edward Stanley of Wood Hall, Reddish.

Edward Hyde gained recruits from the tenantry of William Davenport of Bramhall Hall, whose supper was disturbed by the presentation of a petition from twenty-four of them, begging him to lead them in defence of parliamentary rights. As Davenport had already shown his Royalist sympathies, this was unlikely, so the next day they enlisted with Edward Hyde and marched off to the defence of Manchester.

Above left: Ralph Arderne of Arden Hall responded to the call to defend Parliament as a captain in their army. In this portrait by David Kelsall he is pictured in his uniform with the alarm bell cast in 1642 for the hall.

Above right: A young gentleman who quickly rose to prominence locally was Robert Duckenfield who became a Roundhead colonel and was in charge of Stockport district.

Middle left: John Angier, parson of Denton chapel, now St Lawrence's, was at the siege of Manchester. Colonel Duckenfield and Samuel Eaton are both buried here.

Below left: Robert Hyde of Hyde Hall, Denton, had held out firmly during the siege, convinced by strong puritan principles.

Lord Strange became Earl of Derby on the death of his father, but he continued to position his cannon outside the besieged town. The death must have affected his concentration, as events showed.

John Angier, parson of Denton chapel, who was in Manchester during the siege, describes the artillery as, 'roaring, thundering, terrifying cannons, whose wide mouths shot forth great bullets weighing between four and six pounds... We heard the report (sound) of them and our hands waxed feeble'. However the cannon did little serious damage and soon the defenders were joking about them. Lord Derby sent in a summons to surrender on terms, but Robert Hyde of Denton stubbornly opposed these, even though the defenders were low on ammunition. On Saturday morning, at the end of a week of fighting, Lord Derby withdrew his cannon, exchanged prisoners and marched away, leaving the Parliamentarian defenders of Manchester victorious. It was the first significant action of the Civil War.

The scene was now set for the Parliamentarians to establish themselves throughout Lancashire and Cheshire. Regiments were formed from the curiously armed rustics who had assembled at Manchester with gun, pike and pitchfork and Parliament started to pay for a properly armed militia.

Sir William Brereton of Handforth Hall was appointed Parliament's commander-in-chief of forces in Cheshire. Robert Duckenfield raised his own regiment, based in Stockport, and along with Ralph Arderne of Bredbury and Humphrey Bulkeley of Cheadle, they marched to the defence of Nantwich where a battle was fought in January 1644 resulting in a Royalist defeat.

The only Royalist troops to appear so far in Stockport were men under Thomas Legh of Adlington Hall, who had marched that far in an attempt to help Lord Derby in the siege of Manchester. His Cheshire rustics, however, refused to cross the county line into Lancashire and he had to march home! Now local parliamentary committees turned their attention to 'delinquents' – people who had shown Royalist sympathies or actively helped the king's cause.

In December 1642 Thomas Legh was besieged in Adlington Hall by Colonel Mainwaring and taken, surrendering arms for 120 men. In March the following

Below left: Holes in a thick iron-studded door are believed to have been caused by bullets.

Below right: Adlington Hall near Poynton endured several sieges while holding out for the king.

year he narrowly escaped death at the Battle of Middlewich after refortifying Adlington for the king, but actually died on duty as part of the Royalist garrison of Chester a year later. In February 1644, Adlington was finally taken after a two-week siege by Colonel Duckenfield when the defenders were commanded by one of Colonel Legh's younger sons. The estate was then sequestrated (confiscated by Parliament) and only returned to the family twelve years later after a number of heavy fines had been paid.

Wythenshawe Hall, held by Robert Tatton, was also fortified for the king and troops from Stockport surrounded the place. Their commander, a Captain Adams, was actually shot by a woman while sitting on a wall within sight of the house. One of the defenders, 'she entreated for a musket to try and fetch him down and succeeded therein. They carried him off and buried him in Stockport, which is esteemed so vile a place the common saying is "when the earth was made the rubbish was sent to Stockport"' – according to the very Royalist Lady Shackerley.

Colonel Duckenfield then employed cannon to bring the siege to a conclusion. Six defenders were killed, being buried side by side in the garden. Stockport parish registers record: '1644 Feb. Buried Captain Adams slayne at Wythenshawe on Sunday 26th was buried the 27th'. All this fighting may seem incomprehensible to us, but it was a product of Englishmen having read the King James' Bible in English for the first time and a feeling that 'the rich man in his castle and the poor man at his gate' wasn't quite right after all and that free Parliaments were the best way to improve matters for everyone.

Edmund Ludlow, a great Parliamentarian, said: 'the dispute between us ... was whether the King should govern as a god by his will and the nation be governed by force like beasts; or whether the people should be governed by laws made by themselves, and live under a government derived from their own consent.'

There were unpleasant manifestations of these policies on both sides. William Davenport of Bramhall recorded: 'On New Year's Day 1643 Sir William Brereton being about Stockport, Capt. Sankey, Capt. Francis Duckenfield, with two or three troops came to Bramhall and went into my stable and took out all my horses, then drove all they could find out of the Park ... afterwards searched my house for arms again, took my fowling piece, stocking piece and drum (which Sir William had left me) with divers [sic] other things.' He never recovered these or other losses. In May the following year parliamentary troops again took his horses, including his own mount, obliging him to walk home from Woodford, and then quartered themselves at Bramhall Hall. He wrote bitterly:

Next day after they were gone, came Prince Rupert [and] his army, by whom I lost better than a hundred pounds in linen besides rifling and pulling in pieces my house. By whom and my Lord Goring's army, I lost eight horses and besides victuals and other provision they ate threescore bushells of oats. No sooner was the Prince gone but Cornet Lely and twenty of his troop hastened to plunder me of my horses which the Prince had left me, which they did, not regarding the quarter they had before.

Next he was reported to the Commission for Sequestration for 'delinquency',

Above left: Bramall Hall was repeatedly pillaged by both sides, with William Davenport losing horses, food and linen. This is the Tudor bedroom.

Above right: Marple Hall, festooned with ivy, was the main residence of the Bradshawe's of Marple. It was demolished in 1958 and had many strange legends of ghosts.

– by whose malicious instigation I could not yet come to know, but certainly by my own tenants.

The Commissioners 'narrowly searched every corner' of Bramhall Hall, 'causing all boxes and chests to be opened, which otherwise they threatened to break up, being in the meantime guarded by a company of musketeers who stood in the Park and all about the house with their matches lighted (ready to fire).'

After making an inventory of his house the Sequestrators, who included William Siddall, one of his tenants, now a captain in the army, and Major Henry Bradshawe of Marple, summoned Davenport to appear before Colonel Duckenfield who urged him to sign the national Covenant and fined him £500. Unfortunately the local committee had no authority to do this and the National Committee fined him a further £745!

Throughout the summer of 1645 troops quartered themselves at Bramhall – troops of Lord Fairfax's own regiment of horse, General Lesley's Scottish soldiers, who were co-operating with Parliament, and later eight troops of Lancashire horse on their way from deployment in Yorkshire to the siege of Lathom House, the stronghold of the Earl of Derby in Lancashire.

Neighbours of Davenport were similarly afflicted. In addition to the Leghs of Adlington and the Tattons of Wythenshawe, Edward Warren of Poynton, technically still Lord of Stockport, was sequestrated and fined £650. Worse, his wife, Margaret, who was advanced in pregnancy, was stopped in the Park at Poynton riding her favourite pony, by some troopers who rudely ordered her to dismount. The shock induced premature labour and after giving birth to twin sons she died the next day, Stockport parish register recording: '1644 April, buried Margaret, wife of Edward Warren of Poynton Esq. (who died in labour of child)'. It is said that the inscription and memorial on the Easter sepulchre in the chancel at Stockport refers to this incident, which occurred on Easter even. The sepulchre is now occupied by the effigy of Richard de Vernon which was moved there from elsewhere and was originally in a chapel outside the chancel.

The Rector of Stockport, Edmund Shallcrosse, refused to give an oath of allegiance to Parliament and was sequestered, an inventory of goods in his rectory included 600 books and a chest hidden in his wife's bedroom containing curtains and other materials. He was ejected from his living as was the Rector of Cheadle, William Nichols, who fled to the Royalist garrison at Chester and, after its surrender to Denbigh Castle, another Royal stronghold.

It is said that Shallcrosse fell foul of the commissioners because one of them was Henry Bradshawe of Marple, who was in dispute with the rector over rents for tithe lands. Several times, Shallcrosse went to London to plead his case before Parliament's National Committee. On his final journey thither, he and his escort of parliamentary soldiers were attacked by Cavaliers from Dudley Castle and Shallcrosse was killed.

Why had the dispute become so bitter? Initially dogged resistance at Manchester had led to success, but in May 1644 local Roundhead forces had a shock from which they recovered only thanks to Parliament's main armies. On 25 May 1644 Prince Rupert of the Rhine, the king's nephew, led an army of 8-10,000 men towards Stockport, intending to cross by the bridge into Lancashire. This flamboyant cavalry leader was an experienced soldier and the 3,000 local levies which opposed his advance near Cheadle, commanded by colonels Duckenfield and Mainwaring, stood no chance. They had lined the hedgerows with musketeers but Rupert sent in his dragoons under Colonel Washington who raked the hedgerows with their carbines, mounted up and outflanked the fleeing musketeers. The main cavalry then charged and the retreating soldiers fled with the main body, 'entering Stockport pell mell with the enemy'.

Only one soldier is recorded in the parish registers as being buried on 27 May, 'slayne at the taking of Stockport', but reports speak of 'many dead and wounded'. Bullet holes once disfigured the doorway of the old Cheadle Rectory from this conflict and a sword of the period was recovered from the Mersey near Brinksway in the 1940s, perhaps dropped by a fleeing soldier. However it is also recorded that the widow of a local soldier killed at Middlewich lived at Brinksway Banks so perhaps the weapon was his, flung there by a grieving woman who tried to turn her back on war.

Above: A David Kelsall view of Underbank Hall, townhouse of Ralph Arderne, during the Civil War, with troops in the streets.

Below left: An interior view of Marple Hall said to have been dark and gloomy and filled with seventeenth-century furniture and paintings. The robed judge may be John Bradshawe, the Lord President.

Below right: Local Roundheads fled before the experienced troops under Prince Rupert, who drove them into Stockport, capturing their ammunition.

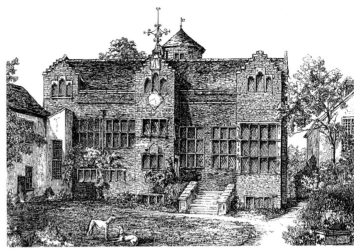

Arden Hall was the scene of a skirmish in the war and a cannon ball was recovered from allotment gardens nearby in the twentieth century.

The Jane Done alarm bell from the hall – a gift by Ralph Arderne's sister-in-law.

Prince Rupert did not linger in Stockport but passed rapidly into Lancashire. A cannonball found near Arden Hall in Bredbury and the name Battle Lane tell of a skirmish there but we have no details other than the legend of 'Cromwell's castle' which as far as can be known he never visited, although his men certainly did. A bell cast in 1642 as an alarm once hung at the hall, the home of Captain Ralph Arderne, and is now in Stockport Museum as a memento of these stirring times. A cottage near Arden Hall, on Castle Hill, also has carvings on beams said to have been made by Roundhead soldiers quartered there.

About 3,000 cavalry under Lord Goring entered Stockport soon after and hurried to join the royal army. Rupert relieved the siege at Lathom House, met up with the Earl of Derby and together they attacked Bolton, where an infamous slaughter of men, women and children took place. Intended to strike terror into the inhabitants of the North-West, it merely led to revenge, as the fortunes of Rupert rapidly changed. At the Battle of Marston Moor near York, he met the combined armies of Parliament and the Scots and after a stubborn fight was utterly defeated. His army and that which had come out of the besieged city of York to join him, was scattered, principally thanks to the skill and tactical organisation of a furious young cavalry officer who was wounded in the battle – Oliver Cromwell.

Religious disputes were very much part of the political scene in the seventeenth century. The publication of the King James version of the Bible in 1611 was intended to promote unification of Protestants but instead it led to division. Even among Puritans there were those who wanted a centralised church government, the Presbyterians, and those who wanted freedom to worship as the mood took them, or as part of the many sects generally termed Independents. Both were united in wanting to get rid of bishops once the Civil War started, just as the bishops had previously wanted to get rid of them.

In 1642 a keen Independent preacher, Samuel Eaton, established the first 'gathered' or Congregational chapel at Dukinfield Old Hall, the home of young Robert Duckenfield. Eaton also started to accompany Duckenfield as his

Elinor Arderne, widowed by the death of Ralph, took comfort from the ministrations of fervent preacher Samuel Eaton, who lived at the hall and often preached there.

Dukinfield Hall and chapel, the home of Colonel Robert and main place of Samuel Eaton's early preaching.

personal chaplain on military duties. Eaton's background was interesting: the third son of a vicar at Great Budworth in Cheshire and educated at Cambridge, he became a preacher but was expelled from West Kirkby by the Bishop of Chester and sought refuge with other Puritans in Holland. After a return to West Kirkby he was again hounded and sailed to the Puritan colony of New Haven in North America. Returning in 1640 to recruit fellow colonists, he was caught up in the political tumult. In 1641 he preached in St John's church, Chester, stating: 'Supreme power in church matters under Christ is in the congregation itself.'

Eaton and Duckenfield accompanied Sir William Brereton on his campaigns in the years 1643-46, when Timothy Taylor was left in charge at Dukinfield chapel, but the whole point of gathered churches was that they were where the worshippers happened to be. In the case of the army, this could be anywhere and their preachers went with them. This was rank heresy to other Protestants.

Curiously, Henry Bradshawe, at one time a major in Duckenfield's regiment, showed his Presbyterian sympathies by unsuccessfully petitioning for the suppression of gathered congregations in 1646.

Eaton quickly became the most influential Independent preacher in Cheshire, writing to Brereton to 'adhere to God and his cause ... and honour those that fear the Lord'. He attributed Sir William's military success to divine favour.

In 1646 occurred the curious incident of the phantom drummer of Dukinfield chapel. While Eaton was preaching, a beating drum was heard to approach, enter the chapel and proceed down the aisle, but no one was seen. The congregation fell to prayer and the sermon was abandoned. Opponents said that this was an omen that the Independents were 'greedy for a war that would prove their ruin'. George Fox, founder of the Quakers, also preached his first sermon there in 1647. Dukinfield chapel still stands in a ruinous state, though the hall once attached to it is long gone.

In the early 1650s Eaton had established Independent churches at Stockport and Chester and moved his base to the old grammar school in Stockport. He was summoned to Scotland by General Cromwell during the campaign there and received a reward. But he was in doctrinal disputes over the Holy Trinity with the elders of Dukinfield chapel. He spent some time with one of Cromwell's chief lieutenants, General John Lambert, who tried in 1660 to prevent the Restoration of Charles II and, this failing, Eaton was ejected from his position at Stockport in 1662. He lived in Bredbury at either Goyt or Bredbury Hall, preaching occasionally at Denton chapel with the permission of the minister, John Angier. He died and was buried at Denton in 1665.

Richard Baxter, speaking of these Puritan ministers wrote, 'so great was the benefit above the hurt which they brought to the church, that many thousands of souls blessed God for them'. He believed that the lasting benefit of the Commonwealth period was the 'true Christian teaching' instilled into the nation by fifteen years of faithful ministry.

Eaton's patron, Robert Duckenfield, was only twenty-three years old when the war began. Sir William Brereton was his godfather, his own father having died in 1630, and the two staunch Puritans went to war together. After their temporary defeat at the Battle of Middlewich in December 1643, a satirist commented: 'Sir William Brereton is fitter to lead a flock of geese than a band of soldiers and that Colonel Duckenfield is but a boy'. But so far from disaster they went on to conquer. Duckenfield fought beside his godfather at Nantwich, when the Royalist forces, including soldiers from Ireland, were routed. He was at the siege of Beeston Castle and was governor of the suburbs of Chester during the siege there, while Brereton was away.

After Sir William's return to Parliament, Duckenfield became military governor of Chester Castle and in 1648 when the second Civil War broke out, he was made commander of all parliamentary garrisons in the North-West and in the following year, High Sheriff of Cheshire. Both he and Brereton were called as commissioners to sit on the trial of King Charles , but were unable to attend. In October 1651, sailing with a fleet of ships, Duckenfield captured the Isle of Man, a stronghold of the Earl of Derby. In the same year he called the court martial which condemned Derby for his part in the massacre at Bolton. The unfortunate earl went to the scaffold with great composure and was beheaded in the Market Place at Bolton, pitied by the spectators. A tankard he drank from before execution used to be exhibited in the Old Man & Scythe nearby and his bloodstained collar was one of the family heirlooms of the Prescots, rectors of Stockport in the nineteenth century.

In 1653 Duckenfield became a member of Cromwell's Parliament, but the bickering of politics in the capital seems to have disillusioned this plain soldier from the shires. He waived the chance to become a member of the Lord Protector's Council of State and the following year he resigned as an MP and relinquished his command at Chester. In March 1655 he wrote to Cromwell personally, stating: 'I should be glad to serve your lordship in any foreign war within the continent of Europe, rather than within this nation'. After Cromwell's death Duckenfield was active again, helping the election of radical Republican John Bradshawe, and raising a troop of horse to defeat Sir George Booth's Royalist rebellion.

After the Restoration of Charles II, Duckenfield was regarded as a dangerous radical and hid for some time in a coal mine on his estate. In 1665 he was arrested in London and held firstly in the Tower and later under house arrest in the Isle of Wight for several years. He returned home after the death of his first wife, Martha, in October 1669. She had borne him eight children. He remarried in 1678 and had a further six children by his second wife, Judith. Duckenfield died in September 1689, just after the Glorious Revolution, which saw the last of Charles I's sons kicked out of the country. Colonel Duckenfield, the associate of Cromwell and General Brereton, was buried within the chancel of Denton chapel, now the Church of St Lawrence. His grave is unmarked.

Cromwell dictating to his secretary, John Milton, in a painting now at Abney Hall, Cheadle. He offered Duckenfield a place in his Government.

December: 1602
John the sonne of Henrye Bradshaw
of Marple was baptized the: 10ᵗʰ   traitor

John Bradshawe, the Lord President who tried King Charles, and his entry of birth in Stockport parish registers, with the word 'traitor' added in a later handwriting.

By far the greatest and most notorious local individual to emerge from the Civil War was John Bradshawe, a younger brother of Henry Bradshawe of Marple. He was born either at a small cottage called 'The Place', or Peace Farm at the bottom of Church Lane in Marple, or at Wybersley Hall, High Lane, both of which were occupied by his father. The Place is now gone, replaced by a petrol station adorned with a blue plaque presented by Stockport Heritage Trust. At the time of writing, Wybersley Hall still stands in a ruinous state and hidden by trees, but plans to restore it are in progress. This was John's boyhood home and from here he set out on a life's adventure which would take him to the highest office in the land.

The Bradshawe's were a yeoman family, a cadet branch of the Bradshawe family of Lancashire which boasted some knightly ancestors. John's brother Henry fought at the Battle of Worcester where he commanded his own regiment of local men and was wounded in action. There is a legend that a niece of Colonel Bradshawe loved a cavalier and that after visiting her at Marple Hall the young man was treacherously drowned in a deep pool of the River Goyt nearby, but this is hearsay. The hall was demolished in 1958 after suffering from vandalism – all that remains are some foundations, a datestone and stories of ghosts. What is known is that, after a career in law, John Bradshawe was selected to preside at the trial of Charles I in Westminster Hall in January 1649. The king sat facing Bradshawe across a long table bearing the parliamentary mace and the sword of state. Row upon row of commissioners, who were to judge Charles, sat behind Bradshawe, also facing the king, with their hats on and soberly dressed. Under his robes the President of the High Court of Justice was wearing armour and on his head an armoured hat to protect against assassination.

Charles behaved with dignified arrogance in the face of his enemies, denying the validity of the court to try him or, indeed, anyone else. Bradshawe insisted that the law was the king's superior and that the people were the authors of the law and Parliament was their protector. 'And truly sir, you have written your meaning in bloody characters throughout the kingdom'. When the sentence 'that Charles Stuart being adjudged a tyrant, traitor (etc.) ... should be put to death by the severing of his head from his body' was read out, sixty-seven commissioners stood up behind Bradshawe, to testify their assent. The king tried to speak, but was ushered from the court, Bradshawe stating significantly, 'Your time is now past'.

Two days later Charles was executed on a scaffold outside his own Palace of Whitehall, and the office of king was abolished as 'unnecessary, burdensome and

HMP

Far left: Poor Charles defended himself with dignity against his accusers, denying their authority to try him or any man!

Left: Unhappy Charles was sentenced by Bradshawe to beheading. His ghost was said to ride round and round Marple Hall on moonlit nights.

dangerous to the liberty, safety and public interest of this nation'. England was declared 'a free state or commonwealth' to be governed by the representatives of the people in Parliament. Bradshawe became the first President of the Council of State and remained so until it was dissolved by Cromwell in 1653. For nearly five years John Bradshawe, the yeoman farmer's son, had been the chief officer of the Commonwealth of England. The republic was renewed briefly after the death of Cromwell, who ruled as Protector until 1658, when Bradshawe was again called upon to be president, but he was already ill.

One newspaper stated: 'This day (31 October 1659) it pleased God to put a period to the life of Lord President Bradshawe after a year's lingering under a fierce quartan ague, which could not have taken him away yet awhile, had he not wasted himself with extraordinary labours from day to day. For the Commonwealth he always lived and for the sake of the Commonwealth he died so soon.'

President Bradshawe was buried with pomp in Westminster Abbey but, following the Restoration of Charles II, he, along with Cromwell and General Ireton, was disinterred from the abbey and their corpses displayed on the gallows at Tyburn, the heads lopped off and set on spikes at Westminster Hall. Thus ended the grand experiment in Republicanism.

On his deathbed, Bradshawe had avowed: 'I acted honestly for the good of my country and had it to be done again, I would be the first man in England to do it!' The poet John Milton, said to have been a kinsman, wrote: 'He assisted the deserving to the utmost of his power. If the cause of the oppressed was to be defended, if the favour or violence of the great was to be withstood, it was impossible to find an advocate more intrepid or more eloquent – one no threats and terrors, and no rewards could seduce from the plain path of rectitude.'

Chapter 5

Jacobites

The last of the Stuarts, Bonnie Prince Charlie, came marching through Stockport with his army of Highland Scots and a few English and Lowlanders in November 1745, just over a century since his relative, Prince Rupert, had done the same. He was considerably more charming than his heavy German cousins, the Hanoverians, who sat on the throne of England, or Great Britain as it had become by the Act of Union with Scotland. But he was constitutionally unacceptable, being like his grandfather, James II, a Roman Catholic and a member of the exiled clan of Royal Stuarts.

Peter Legh of Lyme Hall was among Cheshire gentlemen who were imprisoned in 1715 for trying to help his father, James Edward, the Old Pretender, regain the crown lost by King James. Thirty years later the twenty-five-year-old Charles Edward, now known as the Young Pretender, had landed on a remote Scottish island, gathered the clans, captured Edinburgh and defeated an English army at Prestonpans. Carlisle fell and the rebel army reached Manchester on 28 November, en route for London. Three hundred English recruits were formed into the 'Manchester Regiment' and ten rebel soldiers, known as Jacobites, crossed the Mersey into Stockport, proclaimed Charles, but finding no further recruits quickly left, warning that their army was on its way.

Only the day before, a party of soldiers from the Liverpool Royal Blues Regiment had arrived in Stockport to destroy Lancashire Bridge over the Mersey to slow the rebels' progress south. A correspondent wrote: 'We are all in the utmost confusion here, all the bridges of the River Mersey being ordered to be destroyed ... the principal inhabitants are retired with their best effects from Manchester.'

After scouts had examined the fords, the rebel army cut down trees which they covered with planks to make bridges for their cavalry and artillery at Gatley and Cheadle. The prince crossed with his infantry at Stockport ford, 'which took him up to the middle'. He was dressed in a light plaid, belted about with a blue sash. He wore a grey wig, with a blue bonnet with a white rose in it, and 'it was observed that he looked very dejected'. Most of his men were said to be very ordinary, only his own regiment showed a tolerable appearance. They were armed with guns and pistols, but some only had swords and Highland

shields appropriately known as targets. The artillery train consisted of thirteen field pieces of two- and four-pounder cannon. Some of the army camped in Tiviotdale, said to have been named by the Jacobites because it reminded them of the valley of that name in the Lowlands of Scotland. Fields in Reddish near the Bulls Head were named Blue Bonnets after the headgear of the Highlanders. The ford where they crossed over the Mersey was described by an elderly eyewitness as having been above Mr Marsland's works (near today's Sainsbury's).

A touching scene occurred on the Cheshire bank of the river in Stockport, where a little band of elderly sympathisers, but no recruits, had gathered to welcome the prince. One, an enthusiastic old lady called Mrs Skyring, had sold all her jewels and plate and every little valuable she owned and brought the money in a purse, which she laid at his feet and as she looked at him exclaimed: 'Lord! Now lettest thou thy servant depart in peace!' As a girl she had witnessed the return of Charles II from exile and believed that now, at the end of her life, she was witnessing a similar happy restoration. For years she had sent half of her income to the exiled royal family and concealed her name from them. Her own father, an ardent cavalier, was rumoured to have been basely treated by Charles after the Restoration, but this had not dimmed his daughter's enthusiasm for the Stuart cause.

The rebel army marched on via Macclesfield, where the mayor was forced to proclaim the Pretender and troops were billeted about the town. At Derby Charles was advised by his Council of War that despite its astonishing progress his little army of 7,000 could not reach London without being trapped and probably defeated by two converging Hanoverian forces. The prince urged them on, but the leaders would not be swayed, a general retreat began and by the 8 December straggling groups of rebels were re-crossing the Mersey heading north. One group belonging to the Manchester Regiment was shot at by the night watch as they crossed the ford at Stockport, killing one horse. When the rearguard arrived, commanded by Lord Elcho, they dragged the constable from hiding under a shop counter and put a noose around his neck and the necks of several other hostages, threatening to burn the town if a similar incident occurred. Several townsmen were injured by swordcuts and had their shoes stolen.

Above left: The Highland army encamped about Stockport watch as Mrs Skyring makes her generous but ultimately futile donation to Prince Charles Stuart in this imaginative view by David Kelsall.

Above right: Bonnie Prince Charlie was winsome and charming, but he didn't look very happy when he came to Stockport, wading through the chilly Mersey in November because the bridges had been blown up!

That night Lord Elcho and the prince's Lifeguard quartered around the Market Place, his lordship and, it is rumoured, the prince himself, sleeping at Woodalls, next door to Staircase House. Their horses were stabled in Royal Oak Yard, off Little Underbank. The next day they departed for Manchester, taking six hostages with them, including the constable with a halter round his neck.

On hearing of the prince's retreat, old Mrs Skyring, who was nearly ninety, died from the shock. She was not the last casualty from among the prince's supporters. At Carlisle a garrison was left behind consisting of 120 men of the Manchester Regiment, who with some others held out for eleven days against the Duke of Cumberland's Hanoverian army. After the surrender many of these men, including all the officers, were to suffer the appalling death of hanging, drawing and quartering and the heads of Thomas Deacon and Thomas Syddall were exhibited at the Manchester Exchange.

The bells of St Mary's parish church in Stockport were rung for two days after the Government army passed through in pursuit of the rebels and they rang again in celebration of the prince's final defeat in April 1746 at the Battle of Culloden. A poignant reminder of this interlude in Stockport's history is the corroded but still very sharp Jacobite sword fixed firmly to the wall of the Lady Chapel in St Mary's church, abandoned by a rebel soldier.

The remainder of the eighteenth century was occupied by a series of wars around the globe against the French and then our American cousins, who declared their Independence in 1783. It is said that French prisoners of war were employed to dig the first water tunnels through the soft sandstone rock to supply the early mills in Stockport with waterpower.

The high taxes imposed to pay for the wars caused resentment and one local farmer, Jonathan Thatcher, living at Woodbank, near Offerton, expressed his dissatisfaction by riding his cow, saddled and bridled, to and from the market at Stockport on 27 November 1784. This was his protest against the tax on saddle horses and was made the subject of a famous cartoon, showing the Cheshire farmer outside the Sun Inn, at the junction of Mealhouse Brow and Lower Hillgate. It is said that copies reached the hands of the prime minister, William Pitt, making Thatcher a national celebrity.

Right: Royal Oak Yard beneath Petersgate Bridge and behind the Queen's Head pub was traditionally the place that the Jacobite cavalry stabled their horses. The bridge would not have been there.

Far right: Jonathan Thatcher outside the Sun Inn at the foot of Mealhouse Brow, riding his cow to market as depicted in an eighteenth-century cartoon. A very practical, humorous protest against a tax on horses.

Chapter 6

Early Industry

Our earliest evidence of industry in Stockport comes from the Macclesfield Eyre Rolls – court proceedings for the Macclesfield Forest district, which names Simon le Webster (weaver) and William le Walker (fuller) as textile workers in the 1280s.

By the early eighteenth century hatting, button-making and silk-yarn spinning was established and the first silk mill was built in The Park near Warren Street in 1732. It was erected close by a logwood mill and the manorial cornmill, which were both water powered from a mill leet drawing water from the River Goyt. Fine silk yarn was manufactured on water-powered machinery based on a design by John and Thomas Lombe and introduced to Stockport by a former employee of theirs, an Italian, John Guardivaglio.

The Park silk mill was the first water-powered textile mill in the North-West and it was not until 1759 that the next was built on Carr Brook near Hillgate, followed by Adlington Mill on Tin Brook (near the present post office) which was built in the 1760s. Later silk mills included Crowther's mill across the Mersey in Heaton Norris and another at Cheadle on Micker Brook. A variety of smaller mills with hand-operated or horse-driven machinery also sprang up and by 1769 it was estimated that 2,000 people worked in Stockport's silk industry.

In the 1770s recessions struck the silk industry due to foreign imports and layoffs and bankruptcies caused manufacturers to turn to cotton. The spinning and weaving of cotton had traditionally been a cottage industry, with loomshops – lofts or outbuildings housing hand-operated wooden machinery for spinning and weaving woollen, linen or cotton cloths. William Radcliffe commented that in his home village of Mellor in 1770 only six or seven out of fifty or sixty farmers were not engaged in textile manufacture. The rest were farmers merely during the harvest and weavers more or less full-time.

The invention of the spinning jenny by a Blackburn weaver, James Hargreaves, greatly increased the production of yarn by 1770 and the process was refined by Richard Arkwright's carding engine, which combed the fibres. Radcliffe remembered that old spinning wheels in his native Mellor were all slung into

William Radcliffe, early cotton entrepreneur, went from weaver to master.

Castle mill can just be seen below the church tower in this engraving of Tiviot Dale chapel in 1826 with a passing stage coach heading up Lancashire Hill.

lumber rooms and replaced by jennies at this period. Slowly, small cotton manufactories powered by horse engines or water began to be established in and around Stockport.

The Castle Mill, built to an elaborate and eccentric design by Sir George Warren, lord of the manor of Stockport, was erected on the remains of the old castle mound in the Market Place, as the town's first water-powered cotton muslin mill. It was built to look like a battlemented tower and was oval in shape with an open inner courtyard. A vast wheelpit, recently uncovered during redevelopment of the site, housed a 40ft-diameter undershot waterwheel, fed by a series of water tunnels from higher up the River Goyt. Sir George removed the remains of the medieval castle foundations to erect his mill, which was completed in 1778 and described as looking like 'the grandest prison in the world'. The Milne family who operated the mill for Sir George apparently sold the trade secrets of Arkwright's system of manufacture to France with whom England was then at war! The mill was not a success and ceased manufacture in 1800 after the water power was cut off, when it became a storage area and public house.

Coal mining also took off in eighteenth-century Stockport and district. Richard Arderne of Arden Hall, Bredbury, was purchasing coal from a local mine to bake in his brick kiln the bricks used to build the houses of expanding towns and villages as early as 1745. Even earlier in 1707, one mine at Norbury was producing 700 tons of coal a year. Both waterwheels and Newcomen – or 'atmospheric' steam engines – were used to pump water from the increasingly deep mines and the number of men employed as colliers grew.

Sir George Warren was ever a man on the lookout to increase his riches. He taxed the burgesses and inhabitants of Stockport in every way he could and even dug clay from the common land to sell to brick-makers. He had coal mines at Poynton and became involved in a canal-building scheme with a Macclesfield industrialist, Charles Roe. Together they planned to build a canal from Manchester through Stockport, with a Macclesfield branch, in the 1760s, but their scheme was scotched by the Duke of Bridgewater, who saw their plan as a threat to his

Above left and right: The wheelpit of Castle Mill was uncovered revealing remains of a 40ft-diameter undershot wheel mechanism during work on Courts, near Vernon Street, in 2003.

Left: Arden Hall was close to the Bredbury coalmining district which was exploited by Richard Arderne along with other local gentry.

own coal-carrying canal. It is said he disliked Sir George because he had eloped with an heiress, Jane Revell, to whom the Duke had been engaged. It was not until 1797 that a canal from Manchester was built as far as Lancashire Hill.

Between 1780 and 1830 cotton spinning and weaving was the dominant industry of the region and Stockport was second only to Manchester in the amount being produced. Three quarters of the inhabitants were engaged in cotton manufacture. Mills sprang up along the banks of the Mersey. By 1815, at the end of the Napoleonic Wars with France, forty large cotton spinning factories existed. The first major cotton mill complex was created after Henry Marsland astutely bought up land and water rights and the old silk mill in The Park, near the junction of the Mersey and Goyt rivers. After 1792 his son, Peter, took over the town's biggest cotton mill, fed by a series of water tunnels dug through the soft sandstone rock. Peter Marsland was a local benefactor, creating the first reservoirs and public water supply for the town. He spent his wealth in

Above left: Peter Marsland once owned the largest cotton mill in the world at Park Mills, Stockport. A benefactor who built a public water supply, he may have died as a result of injuries sustained in a riot.

Above right: A view of Stockport from Reddish in 1885 shows how cotton mills had grown along the riverside as far as the eye could see.

building his home, Woodbank Hall and Park away from the smoky town, which is now also a public park in Offerton.

In the 1790s a series of weirs were built across the Mersey to raise the water level, with waterwheels in small wings projecting into the river to drive machinery in cotton mills, including the suitably named Weir or Wear Mill, the basement of which still exists. So much water was being abstracted that in summer the bed of the Goyt beneath New Bridge appeared perfectly dry and mill-owners downstream complained of the lack of water! Steam engines were installed in some mills as a standby for low water levels. Thomas Hope, who gave his name to Hopes Carr, ordered a Boulton & Watt early steam engine for Carr Mills in 1797 to be used 'in droughty weather' when Carr Brook ran dry. Many early mills rented out space and Lower Carr Mill had twenty-seven masters employing 250 people. Hope made so much money from rents that he gave up business after six years!

Quarrels over water led to litigation between the Marslands and the Howards, two major mill owners. Peter Marsland constructed a reservoir in Portwood and dug water tunnels from his estate alongside the Goyt at Woodbank. Howard retaliated by building a weir and millrace at Otterspool to abstract water even higher up the Goyt, the remains of which can still be seen. The quarrel was complicated by a love match between the daughter of one and a son of the other! Eventually Howard was allowed to share water supplied by Marsland's tunnel from Woodbank.

Although some yarn was still spun by women on hand-operated spinning wheels at home (hence the term spinster) this was fast being superseded. A Stockport visitor in 1794 wrote that, 'large fires blazed in every house, by the light of which women were frequently spinning'. But a new machine called the mule, invented by Bolton weaver Samuel Crompton, was widely adopted. By 1811 there were 351,000 mule spindles in Stockport, compared with 85,000 jenny spindles and by 1832 there were 416,000 mules and almost no jennies left.

Right: Intersecting tunnels surveyed in 1959. They once carried waterpower beneath Stockport to drive the early mill machinery.

Left and below: Grand entrance gates to Woodbank Park pictured in the 1920s and Woodbank Hall in the 1980s, the home of the Marsland family away from the smoky mills of Stockport, now part of Stockport Museum.

The earliest cotton factories were multi-storey rectangular blocks with a multitude of large windows, between three and six storeys in height. Samuel Oldknow first established warehouses on Higher Hillgate in the late 1780s, originally employing outworkers to weave his muslin and calico cloth, but by 1790 he built Hillgate Mill, four or five storeys high, arranged around a central courtyard and entirely powered by steam. He lived in the plain Georgian house next door, which still stands. Already, in 1786, Oldknow was the leading manufacturer of muslin in the country. Bleaching and dyeing were added at his works in Heaton Mersey, where many of the original workers' cottages remain on Vale Road, although the works, like his Hillgate Mill, have disappeared. But his biggest impact was on Marple, where he built Mellor Mill and a turnpike road from Stockport, remodelling the entire village. In the 1790s he was the major shareholder in the construction of the Peak Forest Canal. He had a large house beside the Goyt in Marple and employed scores of orphan apprentice girls who lived in nearby Bottoms Hall, known as The Orphanage.

Above left: Samuel Oldknow, industrial entrepreneur who built roads, canals, mills and bleachworks in addition to most of Marple village.

Above right: The eighteenth-century house on Hillgate, Stockport, from which Oldknow began his industrial enterprise, later Christy's Hatworks office.

Right: A model of Mellor Mill by Tom Oldham, showing Oldknow's country house (right) near the bridge over the Goyt.

Powerlooms for weaving cloth started to take work from handloom weavers by the 1790s and two Stockport manufacturers, William Horrocks and Peter Marsland, were using them by the 1800s, incorporating features introduced by another local man, William Radcliffe. From 1822 to 1832 the use of powerlooms increased from 1970 to 11,003 machines and firms began to combine both spinning and weaving operations. In 1825 there were sixty-two steam engines powering Stockport cotton mills. The buildings began to be built of fireproof materials, using cast-iron beams instead of wood and stone-flagged floors. Wellington Mill, built in 1828 by Thomas Marsland, had cast-iron roof trusses, iron beams and brick vaulting, and a workforce of 947 – the largest in town. The mill can still be seen, as it now houses Stockport's museum of hatting. Orrell's Mill, on Travis Brow, Heaton Norris, surpassed this in 1834 with a workforce of 1,264.

Mill owners began to build housing for their workers. The Andrew family at Compstall built a church, library and country estate with coal mines in the woods and a canal to transport it to their mill in the 1820s. The Gregs, who created the mill at Quarry Bank near Styal, now owned by the National Trust, built mills alongside the canal in Reddish, and William Houldsworth created a model community near his impressive mill in the centre of the village.

Two views of Wellington Mill – one from Wellington Road viaduct in the 1990s and the other by David Kelsall in about 1845.

Stockport hats at the wedding of Harry and Lily Coop in 1900.

Hillgate was Stockport's hatting district viewed here in the 1960s, with the cooling tower and gasometer still standing in Portwood.

Hatting was also growing and in 1826 Christys, a London firm, bought out Worsleys, a Stockport company and by 1840 had erected a five-storey warehouse. They also took over Samuel Oldknow's former cotton mill on Hillgate and his house was used as their offices. Stockport became famous for its hats – Wellington Mill becoming part of Ward's, the Bredbury hatting company.

Modern Stockport could be said to have arrived with the railway. A turnpike trust had built the Wellington Road viaduct in 1826, providing the town's first bypass and an alternative route to the traditional Hillgate coach route into the town centre, lined by coaching inns. Old coaching routes were to become a thing of the past and places like Bullock Smithy, which had grown fat on the coach trade, with its infamous cockfights and raucous beerhouses, faded from memory. The construction of the railway viaduct in 1839-40 was the largest civil engineering

The main turnpike road through Hazel Grove, now the A6, in the late nineteenth century was an old coaching route, lined by inns and rough characters.

A horse-drawn outing from Heaton Norris in the 1900s, with very lean horses in the shafts.

project yet, utilising eleven million bricks in twenty-six arches which spanned the Mersey Valley. The Manchester and Birmingham Railway Company had decided to link their two cities and the route came through Stockport. The first station was built in Heaton Norris, on the Lancashire side of the valley and completed in 1840. Trains finally crossed the viaduct with fireworks, brass bands and celebrations, in May 1842. The next year Edgeley station was opened and became the principal entrance to Stockport, its goods and people. Travellers found the arrogant coach driver, who demanded tips from his customers, and the drunken ostler of the inn yard replaced by the courteous ticket clerk and helpful railway porter.

Railways continued to criss-cross the borough, expanding industry and creating a major source of employment with 2,400 railway employees by 1931. Hatting also took off in the 1860s with Christys, Battersbys and Wards, leading the way with felt hat manufacture. A dozen large hatting concerns employed about 4,000 people at the end of the nineteenth century. But engineering had become a bigger employer for local people, initially supplying metalwork for the textile industry. Craven Brothers moved to Reddish in 1900, building cranes and making machine

The railway viaduct crossed the Mersey Valley in 1842 making travel to Birmingham and London possible. It was widened into four tracks in the 1880s using giant wooden formers to built the brick arches.

tools. James Mills established Bredbury Steelworks in 1874 and Simon Engineering came to Cheadle Heath in 1926. In 1908 Mirrlees started to manufacture diesel engines at Bramhall Moor Lane. During the First World War the country's second national aircraft factory was built in Heaton Chapel, run by Crossley Motors Ltd; fifteen acres in extent and employing 2,500 people, it assembled over 400 de Havilland fighters. By the Second World War the Heaton Chapel factory was run by Fairey Engineering and in 1943 the employees had risen to 15,000, building a variety of aircraft. At Woodford aerodrome, opened in 1925, another company, Avros, designed and built the Lancaster bomber, equipped with Rolls-Royce Merlin engines, perhaps the most famous heavy aircraft of the Second World War. Up until 1945 over 4,100 had been assembled by a workforce of 3,000 – seven Lancasters coming off the production line every day. Lancasters dropped more bombs than any other British aircraft and their exploits in sinking the battleship *Tirpitz*, and in the Dambusters raid, are legendary.

Tiviot Dale station had attractive colonades and Dutch gables.

A steam train prepares to leave Tiviot Dale station in 1961.

Tracks are torn up behind the last train to leave Tiviot Dale cutting in 1983.

Chapter 7

Industrial Unrest

The end of the eighteenth century was a very uncertain period. Handloom weavers working at home in weaving sheds and lofts were being superseded by small factories, situated on streams where water power could turn the looms by a series of pulleys driven by a waterwheel. There was no shortage of orders for textiles. Armies and navies needed clothing – even Napoleon's soldiers wore British cloth and marched in British boots despite his attempts to exclude English goods from a Europe dominated by France.

By the 1800s weavers were asking for higher wages and in 1808 a master spinner of Stockport called Dawson addressed a crowd on Old Road, Heaton Norris, urging them to persist in their just demands. The poor weavers next found a champion in the person of Colonel John Hanson of Strangeways Hall, Manchester, who spoke to a mob estimated at 70,000. He, like Dawson, was sentenced to jail for six months, but on his return to Stockport, the grateful weavers unhitched his horses and drew his carriage along by hand and later presented him with a gold cup. He died aged thirty-seven from heart disease, brought on by his sojourn in prison. The Government and magistrates were determined to suppress any movement of a revolutionary character and offered rewards to apprehend agitators, including a schoolmaster from Old Road, John Sharp, who fled to escape arrest.

The year 1812 saw the murder of a prime minister in the lobby of the House of Commons, shot by a disgruntled merchant, and the birth of the Luddites – sworn to destroy machinery which deprived them of work. In March 1812 groups of them entered Stockport, breaking open provision stores and stoning the windows of mill owner Peter Marsland in Heaton Lane. The windows of Constable Birch and the factory of William Radcliffe, the inventor of the dressing frame, came in for particular attention. After they set fire to Edgeley Cottage, off Castle Street, a local magistrate, the Revd Charles Prescot, Rector of Stockport, read the Riot Act and a detachment of Scots Greys, supported by local yeomanry, dragoons and infantry, charged the rioters with drawn swords.

Many were wounded and a large number arrested. Of these, twenty-eight were committed for trial at Chester charged with having set fire to the house of John Goodair, manufacturer, of Edgeley. A total of fourteen were condemned to death, although only two were hanged, eight were transported for life and the rest jailed for various periods. Among these was a woman, nicknamed 'Mrs Ludd' who while in custody at Stockport developed a romantic attachment to her jailor. On her release they were married and she became the mistress of the Stockport 'lock up' where she had once been a prisoner!

The cost of the French wars were beginning to exhaust the country. Trade was bad, harvests were poor and the price of corn – and thus bread – was artificially high. 'Oatmeal and barley bread, nearly black, were the principal articles of food.' Bread made with wheat might be obtained once a month but was so poor that the centre beneath the crust was 'as sticky as bird lime'. Oatcake and porridge with milk and water and an occasional dab of treacle kept the poor alive.

In 1815 Napoleon was finally defeated at Waterloo, but peace, as is often the case, did not bring prosperity – the corn laws kept the price of corn high, to the benefit of landowners and farmers and to the detriment of the working-class poor. The House of Commons, like the Lords, was filled with gentlemen of property. Apart from some radicals, inspired by the revolutions in France and America, or genuinely outraged by social injustice, most members of both Houses of Parliament didn't disturb themselves unduly about the lower orders. Their concern was mainly with keeping the peace and ensuring that the workers in their factories, or on their estates, did as they were told and obeyed the law which their betters had framed for them. Even the radicals had grown wise, harkening to the words of Richard Parker, hanged for demanding better conditions in the Royal Navy during the Nore mutiny. 'The ordinary people will as happily see you elevated on a scaffold as on a rostrum.'

Radicalism in Stockport dated back to the civil wars and in 1792 the Stockport Friends of Universal Peace and the Rights of Man were holding meetings in the Market Place. Other societies followed: the United Englishmen, the Union

Above left: Homes around Lancashire Hill were some of the poorest in Stockport and agitators addressed crowds here. Hanover chapel was built in 1821 and demolished in 1966. The mills and gasometer of Portwood lie beyond.

Above right: The Revd Charles Prescot Jnr. He and his father were active magistrates in the early nineteenth-century industrial troubles.

Above left: Stockport almshouses were just behind St Mary's church and provided a haven for a handful of poor people like this old lady in Victorian times.

Above right: Wellington Road in 1910. By the end of the century work for all and improved social conditions, with trams and bicycles for cheap transport, meant fewer people cared about radical politics.

Society and in 1817 a mass rally of weavers, hatters and other radicals gathered in Manchester intending to march on Parliament with a petition.

Among the Loyalist forces gathered to resist them was Stockport magistrate's clerk, the lawyer John Lloyd, an officer in the Stockport Yeomanry, a troop of thirty-seven local farmers who could supply their own horses to defend the Government. Lloyd was also avid in enrolling special constables, who were to provide their own pistols and ammunition to act in support of the magistrates. There were only two full-time constables in Stockport supported by the jailer of the New Bailey prison, near Lancashire Bridge, who acted as a deputy constable and carried out arrests in the neighbourhood.

When the marchers got to Stockport carrying the blankets they intended to sleep in en route, some were turned back, others waded across the river and a number were allowed to pass, then arrested and herded into the yard of the Castle Inn, Market Place. Some who got as far as Macclesfield were also brought back to Stockport. On Old Road, Lancashire Hill, an innocent bystander, John James, who went out to close his yard gate was sabred across the head by a mounted soldier and died after several days' suffering. Although a jury returned a verdict of unlawful killing against the assailant, he was never identified. Only one 'blanketeer' reached London to present his petition.

Twenty-one were sent for trial at Chester, escorted by the Stockport Yeomanry and three, Bagguley, Drummond and Johnston, were taken to London but, appearing before the Kings Bench, they were discharged on bail for their future good behaviour.

An attack on Hope Carr Mills led to injuries on both sides and a surgeon, Dr Cheetham, helping injured strikers, was shot at by the yeomanry and a special constable, who fired through the door of his house. Incidents of this kind became repetitious during the early nineteenth century. In 1818 the Stockport Union for the Promotion of Human Happiness met in an old windmill on Edward Street, near the present Town Hall. Its leading light was the Revd Joseph Harrison, a nonconformist minister and self-styled 'chaplain to the poor and needy'. Early in

63

1819 radical orator Henry Hunt addressed crowds from an upper window of the Bull's Head, Market Place, and a tin cup, filled with ale, was passed among the crowd, who drank to liberty. Bagguley, Drummond and Johnston had been sent to jail for making seditious speeches and breaking their bail bond and protest rallies were held at Sandy Brow in Stockport near the present-day Stopford House.

John Lloyd attempted to break up one of these and was repulsed with stones and insults. His young son, Horatio, was also attacked by the crowd. Smarting under this, he indicted two of the speakers, Sir Charles Wolseley and the Revd Harrison, and sent two special constables to arrest the men. Harrison was arrested by William Birch at a radical meeting in London and brought back to Stockport. Birch also arrested Sir Charles at his own house, Wolseley Park in Staffordshire. On his way to report to John Lloyd, Birch was confronted in Churchgate near a street called Loyalty Place, by two or three men. When he demanded to know what they wanted, two of the men stepped aside, but the third drew a pistol and shot the constable in the chest at point-blank range.

It was expected that Birch would die, but he confounded medical opinion by surviving with the bullet impacted in his breast bone. A reward for information about his attacker led Pearson, one of the men who confronted Birch, to accuse Jacob McGhinness, a silk weaver of Edgeley.

In the meantime a great meeting was called by the radicals for 9 August 1819 at St Peter's Fields in Manchester and about 2,000 people attended from Stockport. The Stockport contingent marched peacefully and in a gay carnival spirit, witnesses recorded. It was a pleasant summer day and a band played patriotic tunes. Almost as soon as Henry Hunt and James Moorhouse,

Constable Birch is shot by McGhinness in Loyalty Place, just off Churchgate.

1 *Above left:* More recently described as medieval boundary markers, or the round shafts of Mercian crosses, minus their heads, Robin Hood's Picking Rods on Ludworth Moor have many legends. Below the dark and brooding crater of Coombes Rocks, the Picking Rods have played host to Robin Hood (target practice) and Druids (maiden sacrifice) in popular imagination. Who can say – there may be an element of truth in all these tales?

2 *Above right:* Watercolour painting of Arden Hall, Bredbury, in 1881, showing extreme dereliction. Known locally as Cromwell's Castle, it was the home of Ralph Arderne, an officer in the Roundhead army.

3 Colonel Robert Duckenfield surveys the garrisoned town of Stokeport during the Civil War in this painting by local artist David Kelsall. Duckenfield was offered a seat in Cromwell's Council of State, but preferred the life of a soldier.

4 *Left:* Medieval re-enactment group Knights in Battle fought vigorously at the first Chadkirk Festival, Romiley, in 1995, watched by an awe-struck crowd. They used real swords and axes and broke two weapons!

5 *Below:* Bramall Hall in Jacobean times from an engraving of the 1840s. The frontage was later remodelled with pointed gables by a Victorian owner, Charles Nevill, giving its different appearance today.

6 *Left:* Goyt Hall in tranquil setting with duck pond. Built in box-framed Tudor style, it once belonged to a branch of the Davenport family. A motorway extension has been planned and may shatter the peace of the valley.

7 *Below:* Covent Garden in Stockport? St Thomas', Hillgate, has Greco-Roman style and its rector would like it to be used for music concerts. The early nineteenth-century church suffers from vandalism but is in the new Hillgate regeneration area – many new homes are being built just over the road on the old Christy hatworks site.

8 Bridge Street and Lancashire Bridge in 1906. The old Buck and Dog was once notorious for disturbances caused by its military customers and visits by the press gang, who used to forcibly enlist men into the Royal Navy.

9 *Above left:* The White Lion was a coaching inn and had pleasure gardens stretching to the banks of the Mersey. This 1900s view shows Union Road, Little Underbank and Petersgate Bridge.

10 *Above right:* Stockport Market Place after the style of William Shuttleworth, *c.*1800. From left to right: a column of the old market house, the Staircase House block, butchers' shambles and St Mary's old church, replaced in 1813, showing the iron weathercock now on Disley church tower.

11 Thatched House tavern stands on the site of the original, once the town's first dispensary for the sick in the eighteenth century. Rebuilt in mock-Tudor style, it faces the Old Rectory across Spring Gardens and has a cobbled road leading to Hopes Carr.

12 *Above left:* Part of St Thomas' Hospital, once the master and matron's apartments in Stockport Union Workhouse, where the impoverished found shelter. The clock and bells are driven by heavy weights once wound by the inmates.

13 *Above right:* The Arden Arms, built in 1815, has resisted change and retains its authentic atmosphere as a Georgian/Victorian pub, with tiled floors, open fires, an old-fashioned bar and good Robinsons beer.

14 *Left:* Market Place in 1910 showing, from left to right, part of Staircase House, Woodalls (now demolished) where the constable hid from Bonnie Prince Charlie and was dragged out with a halter round his neck, St Mary's church and the covered market.

15 *Below:* A view of Market Place from Petersgate Bridge in 1906, showing an extra bay on the covered market, removed soon after for tramcars. Apart from the clothes, horse-drawn cart, urns, balcony on the produce hall and a few chimneys, this scene is not much different today.

16 *Opposite above:* A scene in Marple Bridge around 1900, showing the Norfolk Arms and another old pub now demolished – not very different from the one Samuel Oldknow would have known when Masonic meetings were held there, or when the murderers of mill-owner Thomas Ashton met to plan their crime.

17 *Opposite below:* St Elisabeth's church, Reddish, designed for a mill owner by Sir Alfred Waterhouse, the architect of the Houses of Parliament. It is hidden away behind Houldsworth Square and is a real gem, with a marble interior modelled on St Mark's in Venice.

The Bridge, Marple

47391.

18 The Bakers Vaults recalls the name of a Victorian proprietor, John Baker, famous for his out-sales of local beer. A curiously shaped building on a spur of land between Castle Yard and Bridge Street Brow, its appearance has changed little over the years.

19 Loyalist volunteers once drilled in the yard of the old Warren Bulkeley, close by the courthouse on Warren Street. Now demolished along with the cooling tower, its façade is preserved on a shop front round the corner in Bridge Street.

20 *Above left:* St Mary's church, Cheadle, built in local red sandstone in about 1530, replaced an earlier church. Inside are stone effigies wearing armour of a previous century and an Anglian cross of Saxon times. St Chad is traditionally thought to have visited in the seventh century.

21 *Above right:* The old Rifle Volunteer, Vernon Park, commemorated a rifle range used by nineteenth-century militia on nearby Warth Meadow. The bridge was built in 1864 during the cotton famine, at the expense of Cephas Howard, using unemployed mill workers.

22 The rector of St Mary's, Roger Schoones, volunteered to go in the stocks owned by Stockport Heritage Trust to raise money for Macmillan Nurses. He got a ducking from stallholders while members of Stockport Heritage prepared to dub him!

23 The White Lion was rebuilt in 1904 but has a licence dating back to the fourteenth century. The cobbled turning circle in front of the inn was recently beautified.

24 Robinsons famous brewery is one of the few independents left – and still run by the same family who founded the company at their Unicorn Inn on Hillgate in 1838. Guided tours of the brewing process can be arranged.

25 *Above left:* A lot of money has been spent on improving the Underbanks recently and St Petersgate Bridge is still picturesque, but businesses in this older part of the town centre struggle to attract customers.

26 *Above right:* Perceived as a 'seedy alleyway', historic Rostron Brow is in a regeneration area and will be redeveloped, with the site of the old Dog and Partridge earmarked for town centre apartments.

27 Recently beautified – the churchyard of St Mary's with a flower ensemble intended to represent hats. The Pack Horse pub, left, and covered Market Hall, right, can be seen beyond, while Stockport Heritage Trust's stocks are just visible round the corner of the church. The small greenhouse structure is a safety cage for an arc lamp.

28 Wellington Mill is the earliest complete cotton mill surviving in Stockport and now houses Hat Works, Britain's only museum of hatting, while the upper floors are private apartments with fine views of Stockport Railway Viaduct.

29 The Goyt flows between the red, rocky edge of Newbridge Lane and Palmer Mill towards the distant tower of St Mary's church on the Market Place. The mill has been demolished, but its lower floor has been incorporated in the new retail unit which occupies the site.

30 *Above left:* The classical façade of the old courthouse on Vernon Street was handsome even before recent refurbishment, and its early nineteenth-century style is reminiscent of American colonial architecture. During industrial troubles Chartists and Radicals gathered outside, while special constables armed with cutlasses stood guard.

31 *Above right:* The 'wedding cake' Town Hall, designed by Alfred Brumwell Thomas and opened in 1908, resembles Belfast City Hall also designed by Thomas and is said to have Renaissance features and draw on the architectural style of Sir Christopher Wren.

32 Dominating the south side of Mersey Square near the bus station, the Plaza opened as a theatre and cinema in 1932 and still enjoys that status today, thanks to the efforts of an enthusiastic 'friends' group who helped re-open and refurbish the run-down shell, which had endured a variety of uses until it was resurrected in 1999.

33 Gone for lunch. An old tractor parked midfield during haymaking on the slopes of Werneth Low, near Compstall, Romiley, one of the rural fringes of Stockport, between Etherow Country Park and Werneth Low Country Park.

34 Overlooking Stockport and the Cheshire Plain, this cross stands on Cobden Edge, a ridge over 1,000ft high. Cobden Edge is above Mellor and has attracted religious interest from ancient times, when early peoples buried their dead here, to the services held here every Easter.

35 A 1900s postcard of Windy Bottom or Roman Bridge over the Goyt at Marple, close by Roman Lakes. Neither are actually Roman as the lakes were made by eighteenth-century mill-owner Samuel Oldknow and the bridge is probably not much older, looking just the same today. The Roman tag was created when the area started to attract tourists in the 1800s.

36 In a small copse on Ludworth Moor, above Marple Bridge, lies this mysterious hummock, believed to be a Bronze Age burial mound. A trial excavation in the nineteenth century revealed cremated bone, but it has never been properly investigated by archaeologists. Perhaps one day Brown Low will reveal its secrets.

37 *Left:* The fine proportions of Abney Hall developed from a rich man's fancy after a visit to the Great Exhibition in London in 1851. In 1857 the owner, James Watts, welcomed Prince Albert, Queen Victoria's Consort, as his guest, the first in a long line of eminent visitors. Soon after, Watts was knighted and became the Lord Mayor of Manchester. His son, also James Watts, was a keen photographer and illustrated many books written by his friend, Fletcher Moss, on visits to old homes.

38 *Below:* Browsing peacefully on the hillside beneath Lyme Cage in the evening twilight, this herd of red deer at Lyme Park are direct descendants of the deer which roamed the old Macclesfield Forest, hunting preserve of the Earls of Chester, and protected by savage forest laws from the bowstring-happy fingers of local peasants.

a Stockport radical, accompanied by Harrison, mounted the platform, a troop of Manchester Yeomanry attempted to force its way through the 80,000-strong crowds to serve a warrant for the arrest of the leaders. They made slow progress and the 15th Hussars suddenly charged into the crowd with drawn sabres, causing a mad panic. In the scrum a special constable was trampled to death and eleven other fatalities occurred while over 600 people were injured, either sabred by the brutal soldiers or crushed.

Of these, forty-six, including eight women, are believed to have come from Stockport and district. One man had part of his skull cut away with a sabre slash, but survived and kept it as a memento! It was later exhibited by Hunt to the House of Commons.

The infamy of this day has lived on in popular folklore as an example of the lengths authority was prepared to go in order to suppress legitimate and orderly expressions of popular political sentiment – in an age when ordinary people had no vote. Because the Hussars were famous for their action at Waterloo only four years previously, the event was satirised as 'Peterloo'. The Stockport Yeomanry officered by John Lloyd were also present, and boasted that they 'cut their way through in style' bringing banners they seized from the crowd back to Stockport, where they were burnt on the Market Place. Lloyd described the attacking of peaceful demonstrators as 'a glorious day at Manchester. We have come back with honour'.

Hunt and Moorhouse were both tried at York and sentenced to prison 'for attempting to change the laws by force'. Moorhouse was a Stockport coach proprietor and Hunt had stayed at his house and been driven to the meeting by him in the morning. Sir Charles Wolseley and the Revd Joseph Harrison were tried at Chester. For their seditious speeches they each received prison terms and Revd Harrison spent five years in Chester Castle, including solitary confinement for reading a copy of the Chester Guardian newspaper a well-wisher had sent him! After his release he spent the rest of his life in Stockport ministering to the poor and preaching temperance. Sir Charles was bound under a surety for good behaviour.

Jacob McGhinness had been tracked down and arrested in Ireland and he was tried at Chester in April 1820 along with an alleged accomplice, James Bruce. Both were found guilty and sentenced to death. McGhinness insisted that Bruce knew nothing of the attempted murder, but simply happened to be there when he fired at Birch. Bruce had his sentence commuted to transportation for life but McGhinness was destined for execution. 'Thank you my lord. A good cure for a pain in the head!' he is said to have exclaimed to the judge on the passing of sentence. He shook hands with the injured constable and asked his forgiveness and wrote a memoir explaining his motives before he was hanged at Chester on 20 April. Special Constable Birch was awarded a pension of £120 a year and often complained of pains in his chest. On his death in 1834 a post mortem examination revealed the bullet still lodged in his breastbone and the grisly relic, along with McGhinness's memoir, is exhibited at Stockport Museum in Vernon Park to this day.

Memoir of 'an atheistical reformer' written by McGhinness while awaiting his execution at Chester.

After a brief rise in prosperity in 1824, trade again plunged into depression with about 8,000 people destitute in Stockport alone, subsisting on handouts of less than two shillings a week. The men were provided with half-price coal, potatoes and soup for themselves and their families in return for labour on various road schemes. These included George's Road in Heaton Norris, named after the new king, George IV.

The other scheme of note was New Zealand Road, which was intended to be called 'Trafalgar Road', but the men who worked on it said they would rather be transported to New Zealand – then a penal colony – than work on it!

But the strike of 1829 set the tone for Stockport's reputation as a hotbed of agitation, which in the opinion of the nineteenth-century historian Dr Henry Heginbotham, dissuaded many industrialists from investing in the town for generations to come. Meetings were held at Sandy Brow and Shaw Heath, near the site of the present Florist Hotel and even the Stockport bellman, or town crier, Whitelegg, was indicted for reading an inflammatory placard and imprisoned for six months.

The strike was caused by a reduction in wages at twenty cotton-spinning firms in the town and cotton operatives, including powerloom weavers, took industrial action involving up to 10,000 workers. Strikebreakers were brought in by manufacturers and a confrontation with authority led to shots being fired.

One of the magistrates was Captain Salusbury Price Humphreys of Bramall Hall. He had come to Stockport following an international incident which wrecked his naval career. As captain of HMS *Leopard* he had fired upon an American ship killing members of the crew and badly damaging the vessel, when Britain and America were nominally at peace. He was under orders from his admiral to stop and search American vessels for British deserters and in fact the *Chesapeake*, which he boarded, did have some as crew. Both he and his admiral were considered to have exceeded their authority and were recalled by the Government.

Humphrey's naval career was more or less over and he settled into the life of a country gentleman, managing the Bramhall estate, marrying an heiress, and becoming a JP. When he and Peter Marsland, the mill owner, arrived with a force of special constables and infantry, they found themselves forced back by a hail of bricks and stones flung by the mob in possession of Wellington Road. Outside Spring Bank Mill Captain Humphrey's naval training took over and he ordered the troops to fire. Peter Marsland had been severely injured by this time and the mill, which employed blackleg labour, was under attack. The Riot Act had been read by the mayor, John Kenyon Winterbottom, and this entitled the magistrates to use what force they deemed necessary to disperse the crowd. Several members of the public were seriously wounded as Humphreys instructed the soldiers to fire high, though miraculously none were killed.

Other disturbances followed, including acid throwing, a particularly offensive form of protest. The son of an owner of Mersey Mills fell victim to this, which could only have been devised by an embittered mind. Attacks on blacklegs followed and three men were sentenced to transportation and another to

Captain Salusbury Price Humphreys of Bramall Hall, naval officer and magistrate, had a firm way with rioters.

The Norfolk Arms, Marple Bridge – formerly the Stags Head – where the conspirators met to plan the murder.

death. Five months after the incident at Wellington Road, Peter Marsland, the proprietor of the world's largest cotton factory who had brought a water supply and gaslight to Stockport, died at the age of fifty-nine and was buried in the family mausoleum at Woodbank Park.

In 1831 a sensational murder occurred in Apethorn Lane on the borders of Hyde and Woodley. Thomas Ashton of Pole Bank, the son of Samuel Ashton who owned two cotton mills nearby, was accosted by three men and shot dead in a private path leading from his home. Rewards were offered for information and it was believed that the amiable young man had become the victim of a fledgling trades union. This was confirmed when the attackers were arrested on the evidence of one of them, James Garside, who implicated two others, Joseph and William Moseley. The three confessed they had met a man who gave them pistols and some money to murder one of the Ashtons. The conspirators met in the Stags Head, Marple Bridge, now called the Norfolk Arms. Beside the canal locks in Marple, they swore an oath never to reveal what happened, holding a knife over each other's head in turn. Curiously, this is similar to a Masonic ritual and the Stags Head was used by local Freemasons. Could the early unions have had a Masonic connection? Days after the murder they were met by a man called Stansfield or Schofield who made them sign a book to say they had been paid for the murder.

Garside had sought to gain his freedom while serving a prison term in Derby by informing on the other two, but the evidence of William Moseley was accepted by the Crown, implicating Garside and his own brother, Joseph Moseley, as the actual murderers. These two were sentenced to death at Chester and William Moseley was acquitted. It was believed that all three had been involved in robberies and violence and at least one other murder in the course of a burglary at Marple. The execution of Garside and Moseley was refused by the sheriffs of both the city and county at Chester and they were sent to London for final judgement.

An earnest appeal for mercy was made by the men's attorney, but the judge was determined to make an example of them and ordered the Marshal of the Court to undertake the execution, using men belonging to the Sheriff of Surrey. Garside and Moseley were brought to a gallows erected outside Horsemonger Lane Gaol on 25 November 1834. They had to be supported to the drop. An eyewitness reported: 'Moseley struggled for a short time; Garside apparently did not die easy, for after being hung for some minutes he drew both his legs up two or three times... The number of persons present was very great, every spot which commanded a view of the drop was crowded to excess. There were a great number of females present.'

It is said that Moseley's father was a respectable employee of the Peak Forest Canal Company, who died heartbroken and was buried three weeks before his son's execution. William Moseley disappeared until 1865 when he applied for admission to the Stockport Workhouse, telling the relieving officer that he had been working as a shoemaker in Carlisle for thirty years. He said they had tossed a coin to see who would shoot, but though the lot fell to him, Garside took the pistol out of his hand and did it himself. The callous murderers received £10 between them. Moseley died ten days after he entered the workhouse in Shaw Heath, at the age of sixty.

Meanwhile the Reform Act of 1832 had made Stockport a parliamentary borough with two seats in the House of Commons. In December of that year a massive gathering of 12,000 people packed the Market Place to hear the candidates nominated. To everyone's surprise a radical was elected: John Horatio Lloyd, son of the man who had relentlessly persecuted their earlier predecessors! The other candidate elected was Thomas Marsland, the Tory mill owner. Lloyd did not last long. In practice he did little to advance radical views in Parliament and was replaced by a Liberal candidate, Henry Marsland, in the election of 1837.

A more violent political movement had been gaining ground locally and nationally. The Chartists brought the country closer to revolution than at any time since the Civil War of 200 years before. In 1835 Stockport had become a Municipal Borough with a Town Council and forty-two local councillors. The town clerk was Henry Coppock, and it became his job and that of the mayor, Ralph Pendlebury, to deal with the Chartists who intended to establish the six points of their Charter 'by force of arms'.

They aimed at votes for all adult males, secret ballots, equal-sized constituencies, annual parliaments (still not achieved!), payment of MPs and an end of a property qualification for members. Torchlight processions into Stockport and inflammatory speeches from the windows of the Bulls Head by their leaders Feargus O'Connor and Joseph Rayner Stephens led to the arrest of Stephens. Further meetings at the Stanley Arms on Newbridge Lane addressed by Bronterre O'Brien further alarmed Coppock, who wrote to the Chartist leaders listing the penalties they faced if they assembled under arms. A national petition to Parliament contained 13,000 signatures from Stockport but was rejected outright. In July 1839 Chartists entered the parish church but

Werneth Low, where the Moseleys and Garside met hours before the murder of Thomas Ashton. From here they had a bird's eye view of the scene of their crime.

The courthouse, Vernon Street, scene of Chartist agitation, and the steps leading from the cells to the dock in one of the courtrooms where the Chartist leaders appeared.

behaved themselves while the Revd K.C. Prescot preached. Soon afterwards the authorities raided the house of James Mitchell, a leading Chartist and, finding arms, arrested him. Quantities of arms were discovered in other houses and seventeen people were arrested. The magistrates were assisted by soldiers from the barracks which had been built in the town and special constables armed with pistols and cutlasses. Scores of armed police surrounded the courthouse on Vernon Street as the Chartist leaders were indicted inside.

Mitchell and others received eighteen months imprisonment for conspiracy. For keeping the peace and not losing his head, Pendlebury became Sir Ralph, and subsequently endowed the Pendlebury Orphanage on Lancashire Hill. As a curious footnote, a sword of 1815 pattern was found in the rafters of the Stanley Arms by the son of a landlord in the late twentieth century and brought into Stockport Heritage Centre in St Mary's church, where it was photographed in about 2000. Was this one of the Chartist's weapons, or was it a memento of an even earlier civil conflict – perhaps Peterloo?

In the summer of 1842 the price of corn had just gone up again and manufacturers decided to reduce wages. Chartist agitators found ready listeners among the working class. It was the bi-centenary of the outbreak of the English Civil War and the anniversary of Peterloo was intended to be marked in a fearful manner on 16 August.

A diarist, Absalom Watkin, recorded: 'Tradesmen fear their shops will be plundered and workers appear to think that a revolution accompanied by the pulling down of the rich would not be at all an evil.' The man who delivered their coal from Stockport told Watkin's wife he would bring no more, that they would have the Charter, that the soldiers dare not fire, 'and that we should see what they would do at Manchester next Tuesday, August 16th, as they mean to attack it from all quarters.'

Before then, on the 11th, an immense concourse of rioting workers armed with bludgeons marched into Stockport by way of Hyde and Compstall. They turned out the workers of Jesse Howard and, passing through Portwood, they stopped Park Mills, pulling out the boiler plugs and stopping the mill engines, despite the remonstrances of the owner, Henry Marsland. At Bradshaw's Mill in St Peter's Square they beat the mill owner, James Bradshaw, and all the mills in the town ceased working. The mob next attacked the workhouse in Shaw Heath, shattering the doors and windows and seizing all the bread and provisions and some money. An hour later the military and police arrived and arrested about fifty of the rioters. The magistrates and town clerk, Mr Coppock, instituted an immediate court, but were interrupted by the arrival of a deputation demanding

A sword of early nineteenth-century date similar to the ones found in arms caches hidden around Stockport by the Chartists.

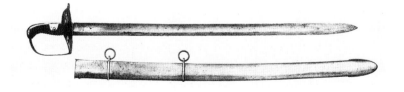

Rioters attacked the Stockport Workhouse at Shaw Heath helping themselves to bread. They were stopped by the arrival of police and magistrates backed by soldiers.

the release of the prisoners. This was refused and as the cavalry was waiting outside with drawn sabres supported by infantry and police, the remainder of the mob backed down. Sixteen prisoners were removed to the courthouse on Vernon Street, which was pierced with loopholes for musketry to defend the place.

The Plug Riots, as they were called, affected all the district around Manchester. By the end of 1842 half the factories in Stockport had closed down, up to 3,000 houses were empty and 5,000 people were, 'walking the streets in compulsory idleness'. Trade unionists had failed to break the manufacturing classes' will by their strike, but they had certainly ruined some of them. Gradually, those workers who still had jobs to go to, returned to work. The Chartist alliance with the Trade Union movement had failed.

Another reform movement had gained momentum with the backing of manufacturers. This was the Anti-Corn Law League. It first started in Stockport in 1838, the year Queen Victoria ascended the throne. The following year it held its first banquet, attended by Stockport members at the Free Trade Hall, built in Manchester on the site of Peterloo. The League had two charismatic leaders, John Bright and Richard Cobden, who believed that the removal of restrictions on imported corn would help the poor by reducing the price of bread and boost the market for their own commodities.

In 1841 Richard Cobden, a successful Manchester textile merchant, was elected as one of the MPs for Stockport. In that year he told fellow members of the House of Commons: 'You must untax the people's bread!' The following year he warned the prime minister, Sir Robert Peel, that there were 60,000 people starving in Stockport and twenty-nine mills stopped in the town. He said: 'If you are not prepared with a remedy, they will be justified in taking food for themselves and their families.' This was not parliamentary language

Above left: Richard Cobden, a young reformer with practical ideas, was a visionary who 'taught the gentlemen of England social economics'.

Above right: Cobden is the only national figure associated with Stockport who earned a statue, pictured in St Peter's Square in the 1900s.

and the prime minister accused Cobden of inciting the people to kill him. Soon afterwards the Plug Riots in Stockport saw starving mill workers break into the workhouse and distribute bread among themselves. Grenadier Guards marched with fixed bayonets through Manchester to quell Chartist riots. It was a wild time, but Cobden and his ally in the Commons, John Bright, stayed cool.

Another Stockport man, John Benjamin Smith, was the first chairman of the Anti-Corn Law League. A visitor reported the hive of activity at the League's London HQ. Scores of clerks were at work sending out propaganda and information to supporters throughout the country. Here was a room full of pamphlets neatly stacked, here another full of printed speeches, others where hundreds of envelopes were being addressed by busy workers.

Finally, in 1846, famine in Ireland forced the Premier's hand. The Corn Laws were repealed and free trade introduced. It wrecked Peel's career and split the Tory party, but Peel attested to the wisdom of Cobden in asserting that this was the best course. Privately Cobden told the chairman of the League, 'the League made them, and you and I made the League'. It was their intelligence and energy in promoting a cause, which had met a stone wall of opposition initially, which mapped out the future of Britain's industrial prosperity. Cobden, in the words of Benjamin Disraeli, a future prime minister, 'taught the gentlemen of England social economics and put cheap bread in the mouths of the poor', for which we and our forefathers must thank him. Cobden left Stockport to represent a Yorkshire constituency the following year. He turned down a baronetcy, saying the greatest honour for an Englishman was, 'to be the chosen representative of a great, intelligent, British constituency'. Stockport remembered him and in 1886, twenty-one years after his death, a bronze statue was unveiled before cheering crowds in St Peter's Square. Carved with the simple inscription 'Cobden', it is the only public statue in the town.

From the end of the eighteenth century Irish workers had been coming over to Stockport to work on the harvest or in construction jobs. They were well established by the 1820s and many of the leading radicals were Irish. But in the 'hungry forties' competition for declining job opportunities in the cotton mills led to rivalry between them and the English. In 1852 an Act of Parliament had prohibited Roman Catholic priests from wearing vestments in public, except in their place of worship. For many years a march through Stockport, by Catholic schoolchildren of Irish parents, had taken place in the summertime. This year it was headed by a large group of Irishmen and the Catholic priest in ordinary, everyday dress. This was assumed by the English to be a provocative demonstration against the new law and in June a fight broke out in the Bishop Blaize pub on Hillgate which soon led to a general mêlée.

The Irish from the district of Edward Street and John Street joined in but were beaten back by English reinforcements. The following evening, on 29 June, they assembled in St Peter's Square, stoned the house of Alderman Graham, smashed the windows of St Peter's schoolroom and attacked people who attempted to protect the buildings with pokers, smoothing irons, sticks, stones and scythes.

The mob made a bonfire of the contents of SS Philip and James Roman Catholic chapel in Edgeley while the priest climbed onto the roof and escaped via a backyard.

St Michael's Roman Catholic chapel just off the Market Place was attacked and never recovered.

An English mob gathered and attacked the homes of the Irish in nearby Rock Row, which was close by the present Plaza Theatre. The inhabitants were dragged from their homes and every article of furniture hurled out onto the street and smashed. A lawless mob rampaged through the town and the Riot Act was read. Dragoons arrived from Manchester and local infantry and special constables were hard at work quelling the rioters.

The Catholic church of SS Philip and James was attacked in Edgeley and the priest, the Revd Randolph Frith, had to clamber onto the roof, then climb down into the yard of the presbytery from where he escaped to the house of a magistrate in Greek Street. Everything inside the church was destroyed, including the organ and a £300 painting of the crucifixion. Frith's library of books was burnt in the street.

Again the mob was confronted by magistrates and police but a portion returned to Stockport and treated the little Catholic chapel of St Michael's at the bottom of Park Street, just off the Market Place, to the same brutal attacks. Previously the town's theatre, it had been a mechanics institute and only opened as a chapel the previous year. Everything inside was destroyed and the building left a shell.

In the fighting one Irishman was killed, mistakenly struck from behind by another with a poker. His attacker, Michael Mulligan, was tried for the wilful murder of the dead man, Michael Moran, but the charge was reduced to manslaughter and he received fifteen years transportation. About a hundred people were injured and sixty-two prisoners were taken by the authorities. Many were discharged but ten English and ten Irish were sent for trial. Two Irish absconded while on bail, while several received up to two years with hard labour.

Although Stockport was spared when further Anglo/Irish rioting occurred in the region, many Stockport public houses had wooden partitions to keep their English and Irish customers apart until the early twentieth century.

The next troubled times occurred in the years 1862-64 when about 10,000 cotton operatives were thrown out of work by the American Civil War, which caused difficulties in getting enough raw cotton from the States to feed the mills in Stockport. A Central Relief Committee was set up staffed by volunteers including the Revd John Evans and the historian, Dr Heginbotham. Coal, clothes and money were distributed and self-help sewing schools for the manufacture of give-away items were set up. Stockport was praised in *The Times* as a model for other towns and cities. In the twentieth century Stockport was affected by the General Strike of May 1926 when workers came out in support of the miners. For nine days the country was almost at a standstill, with volunteers manning buses, delivering goods and even driving trains! The miners remained out for six months and schoolchildren picked over the mining slagheaps in Bredbury for winter coal, while striking miners diverted the River Tame near Woodley to get at the coal seams which broke the surface there, selling the coal they extracted.

Violent clashes between police and strikers made headlines in national newspapers during the Roberts-Arundel dispute in 1967. An American company took over the Chestergate textile engineering firm of Arundel Coulthard and

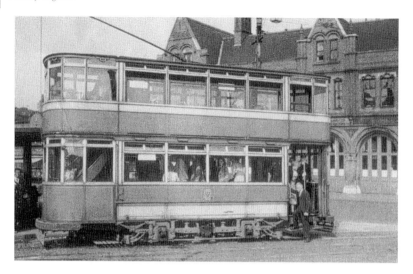

Tramcars, like this one outside the fire station in Mersey Square, were driven by volunteers during the nine-day General Strike of May 1926.

proceeded to ride roughshod over workers' privileges. The AEU declared an official strike and pickets blockaded the factory. A mass march of 3,500 supporters resulted in many arrests and the deputy chief constable, Tom Walker, was among the injured. Lorries carrying goods were chased and stopped at the docks. The strike was over by May 1968 and the firm closed.

In the 1980s a dispute between Eddie Shah and the NGA printer's union led to a siege of the *Messenger* newspapers which he owned, including the free distribution *Stockport Messenger*. New computer technology had revolutionised printing and Mr Shah used non-union staff. Thousands of printers lost their jobs after the Government backed Shah's stance and publishing was radically altered nationally.

Chapter 8

Places to Visit

Bramall Hall

Arguably the jewel of Stockport's places of resort, Bramall Hall (note the dropped 'h') used to belong to the urban district of Hazel Grove and Bramhall, absorbed by Stockport in 1974. It stands in Bramhall Park with a pleasant stream, the Lady Brook, winding past the hall, which occupies a slight eminence, and looks the very picture of the 'black and white' half-timbered halls, for which Lancashire and Cheshire were once famous.

It is now run by Stockport Metropolitan Borough Council and is open to the public, much visited by school groups in which children are able to dress in Tudor costumes and relive life in the time of 'Good Queen Bess' handling artefacts in the kitchen, the spice room and elsewhere in the richly panelled hall.

There is a yearly programme of events – concerts, open-air Shakespeare, opera and themed activities. Victorian rooms are available for hire by companies and the hall is licensed for weddings. It is open for most of the year from 1 p.m. and has car parks and a tearoom in the attractive old stable block.

The oldest part of the hall is constructed of massive timbers resting on a sandstone-flagged floor with no real foundations or cellars, the cage-like structure of the upper timbers giving stability to the whole. The de Bromales were the first inhabitants in the twelfth century. In 1370 the hall passed to the Davenports, who were to hold it until 1829, after which heirs who adopted the name Davenport (including Captain Salusbury Pryce Humphreys) had the pleasure of residing there.

The Davenports were a proud family, adopting the crest of a felon's head with a rope around his neck. Although this was said to signify the power of life and death they wielded as hereditary sergeants of the Forest of Macclesfield, two other speculative traditions existed in the family. One was that a Davenport eloped with a ward of the king and married her without royal consent. He was

The present frontage of Bramall Hall, remodelled by Nevill, with pointed gables.

Tastefully remodelled interior of the chapel room.

condemned to die and only reprieved after the tearful intercession of his young bride with her royal guardian. As a condition of his escape from royal anger he was to wear the crest of the 'thief's neck' on his family coat of arms. The other version was that a Davenport, disturbed at dinner by the sudden entrance of a stranger, ran him through with his sword, only to discover that he had just killed a king's messenger. He escaped by asking the king what a knight should do to defend himself when rudely accosted at his own table by a stranger? The king replied 'Kill him'. Davenport then confessed his crime. The king was enraged, but having himself justified the knight's action and convinced it was an honest mistake (one anyone might make!) simply ordered the Davenports to henceforth wear the badge of 'a rogue's head in a halter' by way of penance.

There are about seventy acres of parkland surrounding the hall, with lakes, lawns, woods and gardens. Trees cut in the nineteenth century revealed ancient arrowheads embedded deep in the heartwood. One of a medieval hunting type with flanges is exhibited at the hall. The medieval ballroom has faded wall paintings of beasts and demons reflecting the close connections with nature and forestry of the former inhabitants. This large upper-storey room, sometimes called the banqueting hall, used to have stained-glass windows with armorial bearings. The central oriel window facing the courtyard has an external fourteenth-century carving of a green man with foliage coming from his mouth. Not far from the hall on Bramhall Golf Course are the remains of an earthwork used as a medieval deer hey through which the deer would be driven once a year to count and control the herd.

Although medieval in origin, the organic growth of the hall put on a big spurt in Elizabethan times. The Paradise, or Dame Dorothy's room, is a fine example of a bedroom of this period, with a Tudor bed, plasterwork and panelling. Dame Dorothy embroidered some bed hangings with the Fall of Man, adding the verse:

> Feare God and Sleepe in Peace
> That thou in Christe mayste reste:
> To passe theis dayes of Sinne
> And raigne with Him in Blisse

It was not always 'blisse' to live at the hall. Davenports of the Civil War period were alternately badmouthed by their tenants, denounced to jumped-up local parliamentary commissioners, and robbed of goods, food and horses by both sides in the 1640s. In addition, both William Davenport and his son Peter had to pay fines to Parliament. After the real Davenport bloodline died out in 1829, poor Captain Humphreys was beset by court cases from a distant Davenport, an ex-soldier of lowly farming background from Woodhouses near Ashton-under-Lyne, who claimed the estate. Fortunately Humphreys had a good lawyer and the claimant, Edmund Davenport, distrained by legal fees, died in debtors prison. Humphreys, though he never went to sea again, eventually became an admiral and died in bed.

Mr Wakefield Christy of the Hillgate hat manufacturing company leased the hall from 1869 and it was briefly repossessed by a putative Davenport in 1877, when the hall and contents were put up for sale. Charles Henry Nevill received the hall as a wedding present from his father, the owner of Strines Print Works. For thirty years he carried out repairs and modifications, restoring old murals, windows and doorways and removing bits not in keeping with the general style. In between, he and his wife, Mary, sailed the world in their yacht *Victoria*, bringing back curios to adorn their unique home.

Bramall Hall before the Nevills' alterations

Charles Nevill who loved a big fish

Mary Nevill, who caught one

John Davies, who died within two years of buying the hall

The old frontage of Bramall Hall and subsequent owners, from left to right: Charles Nevill, Mary Nevill and John Davies.

Nevill loved fishing – so much so that when his bailiff caught the local policeman fishing in the Lady Brook at 3 a.m., the rich man of leisure had his friend the chief constable move the hapless PC to another post and dock his wages by four shillings a week!

The next 'lord' of Bramhall after the Nevills was successful property speculator John Henry Davies. He got onto the boards of several breweries by owning multitudes of off-licences on the ends of rows of houses he had bought. He purchased Bramall Hall when almost no one wanted it and carried out further urgent repairs. He and his wife, Amy, had lived at the smaller black and white Moseley Hall, Cheadle and she returned to live there within two years of the purchase of Bramall Hall.

On the evening of Monday 24 October 1928 the Davies were away in Llandudno. The butler had just phoned them to report that all was well at the hall. He and the servants thought they heard the sound of horses' hooves in the courtyard when the main doors were suddenly blown open by a terrific gust of wind and, as the butler went to lock them, he distinctly heard the sound of hooves die away down the drive. In the morning a stout oak tree in the park was found blown down. That same night, John Henry Davies had died. He was buried in the chapel at the hall.

It wasn't until many years later that the Davies family heard the tale of the 'Red Rider', harbinger of death for the Lord of Bramhall, who rode, according to the legend, 'on a night of storm, with many a tree laid low – when in the morning, the good old knight lay dead'.

There are other ghost stories about jilted lovers, murdered servant girls and the like, but the Red Rider is the oldest and most curious. The Davenports were usually buried in the Lady Chapel at Stockport parish church and more recent burials in the chapel at Bramall Hall have been removed to various cemeteries, since its acquisition in 1935 by Hazel Grove and Bramhall UDC.

Mary Nevill's boudoir, an attic sitting room of homely proportions where she used to enjoy sewing, the servants quarters also in the attic and a working kitchen with oven range, are all recent additions to the hall's attractions.

Lyme Park

The hall and park at Lyme Hall are situated within the ancient hamlet of Dystlegh Dene, once a township of Stockport but now part of the County of Cheshire. The Lyme estate was given to the National Trust by Lord Newton in 1946 but was then leased and managed by Stockport Borough Council until the 1990s, when the National Trust took over again. Described as a 'Palace on the edge of the Peak', Lyme Hall is like a miniature Chatsworth in a superb setting, and has become world famous as 'Pemberley', the home of Mr D'Arcy in the television adaptation of Jane Austen's novel *Pride and Prejudice*.

Covering many acres of moorland hillside and forest, the extensive parkland provides a home to separate herds of red and fallow deer. The larger red deer are actual descendants of the ancient herds which roamed Macclesfield Forest, but the fallow deer, introduced in the Middle Ages, died out in the 1930s and were re-introduced in 1980. There was also a herd of ancient wild white cattle, but sadly these long-horned creatures had also gone by 1900, although a preserved head remains at the hall. Lyme was also famous for its breed of mastiff – enormous hunting dogs which kept poachers of Lyme's abundant wildlife at bay.

Lyme Cage, bulky and forbidding, once a jail for poachers, has been restored and is open on some weekends.

The sense of wilderness pervades the parkland even today. I have a distinct memory of a bright frosty winter morning as a young boy in the 1960s, walking through the forest at Lyme with my father and discovering, stretched out in a hidden hollow, away from well-trodden paths, the recently-dead carcase of a full-grown stag. I can still see the winter sunlight shining on the tips of his magnificent antlers and his black polished hooves. His eyes had gone and little animals had been nibbling at his lips, which were ragged and raw. This was truly a sight from another age, as he lay there in the silent majesty of death, witnessed only by my father and I.

The main entrance to Lyme Park is from the A6 near Disley and cars follow a long, winding drive through parkland until the hall comes in sight. The car park is below the hall and formal gardens near the lake and visitor centre. This area once provided the laundry when the hall was full of residents and their guests. The present estate cottages and restaurant handled laundry sent even from Lord Newton's London residence in large laundry baskets.

Exhibitions at the hall tell of the upstairs-downstairs life of a small army of servants. Descendants of many still live in the Disley area. There are also regular events, including craft fairs, music and outdoor theatre. The park is normally open all day every day in hours of daylight and the hall during the afternoon from April to October.

Visitors will see a large hilltop structure on approaching the park, known as Lyme Cage. It was built as a hunting lodge from which ladies could watch the gentlemen hunting deer on horseback around the park and then enjoy food and refreshment with them when they returned. It was built in 1524 but remodelled by Italian architect Giacomo Leoni in the 1730s. It was known as the Cage from the seventeenth century apparently because poachers were held there pending their removal for trial at Macclesfield. From the 1850s to 1920s it was the home of an estate worker. The unfortunate inhabitant had to fetch water from the bottom of the hill and regularly swill the internal stone staircases from top to bottom! Having a large family with many children to fetch the buckets helped, but the poor souls were also apparently plagued by ghosts! Since a recent refurbishment, the Cage is often open to visitors at weekends and gives magnificent views of the Cheshire plain and surrounding hills.

The Legh family have been associated with Lyme Park since 1388 when Peter Legh married heiress Margaret Danyers, whose father had served King Edward III in France. In reward, Peter Legh was granted a piece of land in the Royal Forest of Macclesfield – 'richly stored with red and fallow deer' – known as Lyme Handley. The hall was originally a hunting lodge in this forest but by 1465 it was described as 'one fair hall with its high chamber'. In 1570 Peter Legh VII built the east and north sides of the present house together with the courtyard porch and a missing south wing. Part of a tower on this Elizabethan hall was removed in the eighteenth century by Leoni and re-erected in the woods as a folly now known as the Lantern, from its pointed turret.

Peter X employed Leoni to expand and modernise the house in the classical style, creating the south front, famous as 'Pemberley' in the televised *Pride and*

Lyme Hall embowered in hills and woods, surrounded by a deer park, is one of the few gentry homes to have survived from the age of medieval privilege – now run by the National Trust.

Prejudice. He also completed the west front, the present courtyard and much of the interior design. The hall had been extended in the previous century by Richard Legh, who did his best to keep out of politics in the Civil War. During this century the dry-stone walling began to replace wooden fences, palisades and hedging – giving the park much of its distinctive appearance of today. A team of rangers constantly repair these walls from damage caused by wind, weather and people.

Among the older parts of the house is the stunning long gallery dating from Elizabethan times, where ladies could perambulate for exercise without leaving the house! It is lined with portraits and has a fine ceiling and panelled walls. One cold winter's night the housekeeper discovered the children of the first Lord Newton pouring water over the floor in the hope that it would freeze and make a skating gallery!

Nearby is the Knight's Room, also known as the Ghost Room; under the floorboards next to the fireplace a skeleton was found which the family believed was that of a priest. A ghostly presence is said to haunt the room. Tradition also states that Mary Queen of Scots stayed in this room and the smell of oranges (she was fond of marmalade) has been noticed here by guides at the hall. In later years only male guests used these bedrooms – the ladies kept well away!

In 1676 another royal guest, James Duke of York, later James II, stayed at Lyme and slept in the Yellow Bedroom. It is said he hunted in the park and killed a buck at Poynton. Lead downspouts at the hall record the visit. Unfortunately James was a bad king and was kicked out of the country by William of Orange at the invitation of Parliament. Peter Legh of Lyme was suspected of 'Jacobite' sympathies as a member of the Cheshire Gentlemen. He suffered the indignity of being tied up in his own house while a Dutch officer sent by William ransacked his private papers searching for treasonable correspondence. Sent to the Tower of London, he was eventually released after his wife wrote to Queen Mary, the sister of James, who had married William and now reigned with him as joint sovereign.

Under the floorboards near the fireplace a skeleton was found in the haunted Knight's Room

Thomas Legh, Peter's brother and an MP, summed up the family policy when he wrote in 1688: 'The cloud of rebellion is very great. It is not safe in this age and juncture of time to meddle in politics and state affairs. I shall hasten to come to that place (Lyme) which God Almighty wonderfully preserved in the late intestine wars.'

And preserved it was, and continued to be, despite Peter X holding meetings of the Cheshire Gentlemen in the beautiful Elizabethan Stag Parlour to plot the return of James II. The room used to have portraits of another unfortunate Stuart, Charles I, and four chairs covered with material from a cloak worn by Charles at his execution. Was this a keepsake from John Bradshawe, their former neighbour and the judge who condemned the king and ordered his execution?

Another treasure of the hall dating from the 1680s are the delicate Grinling Gibbons woodcarvings which now decorate the walls of the Saloon. An atmospheric, heavily panelled Elizabethan room full of ancient stained glass is the Drawing Room. By contrast, the wonderfully light and airy Library, full of ancient volumes, but with high walls and ceiling, was designed by Lewis Wyatt in 1813. Stone stelae or reliefs from ancient Greece of 350 BC decorate the fireplace and compass bay window. They were brought back from a tour of Africa, Greece and the Near East by Thomas Legh. Wyatt also created the elegant Dining Room in the style of the 1680s. The stone wine cooler, once filled with ice collected off ponds in winter and stored, is a feature of the room.

The lake beyond Leoni's south front was once larger than it is today and figures in the popular imagination as the spot where Mr D'Arcy took his dip. But in 1688 it was –tragically – the place where five-year-old John Legh drowned while out playing.

The south front and lake, where Mr D'Arcy did not really swim, but a child of the Legh family did actually drown.

A sunken, or Dutch, garden was created after terraces were built to support the extensions to the hall and planted in its present form by Victorian gardeners. It was restored after a collapse of the terrace in the 1980s. The Orangery, once heated by a furnace, houses three 170-year-old plants – a fig tree and two camellias. Many old-fashioned blooms can be found in the rose gardens and Lyme's unique funnel-shaped scarlet flower, *Penstemon rubicunda*.

Though cool, the air up here is good. Lyme's oldest inhabitant, Joseph Watson the Park Keeper, lived to be 104 and drank a gallon of home-brewed beer a day! He was still hunting at over 100 and once drove twenty-four deer from Lyme to Windsor for a bet! The deep-throated bellow of the rutting stag drifts on the wind from the autumnal hillsides – an ancient sound. And over the forested knoll of Knight's Low a spectral funeral procession is sometimes seen to wind, followed by a grieving woman in white. Legend has it that this is the funeral dirge of Sir Piers Legh, who died in France after Agincourt, but there is so much history here no one really knows.

Marple locks and canals

Still on the rural edges of the borough lies a remnant of the Industrial Revolution which is now a major leisure resource. Narrowboat enthusiasts regularly ply the Macclesfield and Peak Forest Canals around the eastern fringes of Stockport and their gaily painted canal barges may be seen moored alongside marinas at Top Lock, Marple and Higher Poynton.

The Marple flight of sixteen locks stretches for nearly a mile joining the higher and lower sections of the Peak Forest Canal, built by local industrialists in the late eighteenth, early nineteenth centuries. Chief among these was local cotton entrepreneur Samuel Oldknow, under whose land, at Hyde Bank near Romiley, the canal passed in a tunnel. The idea was to ship limestone from the Derbyshire terminus at Buxworth and Whaley Bridge for use in industry.

Top Lock, Marple, on the Peak Forest Canal, has a boatyard and marina and is at the junction with the Macclesfield Canal.

Construction posed considerable problems, with a height difference between the two sections of 60m. A fine arched stone aqueduct, designed by Benjamin Outram, had to be built across the River Goyt, which took seven years and cost the lives of seven workers, opening to traffic in 1800. The upper section had been finished in 1796 and until the locks were completed in 1804 a tramroad transported goods from boats on the higher to the lower section and back. The remains of lime kilns created near Top Lock by Oldknow, to make lime from limestone, can still be seen.

The Macclesfield Canal, now part of the Cheshire Ring of canals, was opened in 1831, linking with the Peak Forest at Top Lock, Marple. A branch of the canal at High Lane provided a transport outlet for goods made by Stockport firms and coal mined at Norbury and Middlewood.

Today these canals provide an idyllic waterside leisure environment and the route of the Peak Forest Canal along the slopes of Goyt Valley near Strines, looking towards Cobden Edge and Kinder Scout, is particularly pleasant for walkers and narrowboaters alike.

Air-raid tunnels, Stockport

Right in the heart of Stockport town centre and burrowing through its native red bunter sandstone rock are the miles of tunnels which sheltered thousands of citizens from Nazi air raids in the 1940s. First excavated when the threat of war became apparent in 1938, they were started after it was discovered that a tunnel 7ft in width and height could be dug without the need for props.

Some houses had been demolished on Chestergate revealing cellars cut into the sandstone cliffs. These were extended at very little cost and two main parallel tunnels linked by nineteen shorter cross tunnels were opened to the public in October 1939. They could accommodate 4,000 people and attracted so many customers from Manchester as well as Stockport that they were

Air-raid shelter tunnels go for miles under Stockport streets and beneath the graveyard of St Peter's church!

extended when the Blitz began in October 1940. They stretched eventually from Lower Hillgate to Mersey Square and other sets of tunnels had been dug at Brinksway, in Portwood and in Heaton Norris.

Regulars at the 'Chestergate Hotel' even booked places and non-Stockport residents had to register with the town clerk. There were as many as 200 'permanent residents', although facilities were primitive, with chemical toilets divided by canvas screens in the cramped, poorly ventilated tunnels. Wooden benches along the sides of the tunnels provided somewhere to sit, later supplemented by 1,000 government-issued steel bunks. Everything was covered in condensation.

By October 1943 the number of regular users had fallen to eight and the Council closed the shelters, ordering that a key be left with on-duty ARP wardens who could open up in the event of a raid. The fittings were left intact after the war and were occasionally inspected by visitors on special tours in the 1980s. It was proposed that the tunnels could be opened as a tourist attraction and, despite initial opposition from some councillors who felt that this might romanticise the horrors of the Second World War, the project went ahead. A reception area guides visitors into the labyrinth of tunnels, most of which are lit and laid out in 1940s fashion, with a first-aid post, sleeping and toilet facilities and catering arrangements. At Christmas, special sing songs are organised and all-year-round tours visit the furthest reaches of the tunnels with torches, led by uniformed guides, to explore the parts visitors seldom see.

The air-raid shelters on Chestergate are open daily from 1 p.m. to 5 p.m. and are the largest purpose-built underground civilian shelters in Britain.

Hat Works Museum

Dominating Wellington Road in the town centre, seven-storey Wellington Mill is an early example of a 'fire-proof' cotton mill. Built by Thomas Marsland in 1828, it used cast-iron beams supporting brick vaulting between floors, then covered with a layer of sand or ash onto which the floor surface, usually stone flags, was laid. This was to prevent fire from spreading disastrously from floor to floor in the inflammable environment of air-borne cotton fibres. As early as 1833 Marsland employed 947 workers both spinning and weaving cotton in this mill – the largest workforce in the town.

Perhaps because of its solid construction, Wellington Mill survived when mills started to become redundant. It even had cast-iron roof trusses. In the 1890s a hatting company, Wards of Bredbury, moved into the mill and sold hats manufactured there from shops in Lower Hillgate and on the Market Place. After the 1940s hatting declined and the mill was split up and used by various small companies. Despite lying largely derelict in the 1980s, the 1990s saw a joyous resurrection as Wellington Mill was transformed into Britain's only museum of hatting.

The upper floors were redeveloped as residential apartments while the middle and lower floors became Hat Works. When the planning application first came before the Council the proposal was to demolish the mill chimney and just

Wellington Mill, which houses Hat Works, can be seen top right of this view, taken when the Prince of Wales came to open Stockport's new Town Hall in 1908.

keep the body of the mill. This was successfully opposed by myself and another councillor, who felt it was important to keep the form of the mill intact. It may eventually be the only mill chimney left in Stockport.

Hat Works has a permanent display of hats and hatting machinery and regularly changing exhibitions, including other items of clothing. Among the items on display have been hats worn by the Duke of Wellington, after whom the mill was originally named, Queen Victoria and Judge Bradshawe, who famously wore an armoured hat at the trial of Charles I. The Level 2 Cafe has fine views of Stockport's brick railway viaduct and there are internet facilities. Hat Works is open from 10 a.m. to 5 p.m. Monday to Friday and during the afternoon at weekends.

Staircase House and Stockport Story

Stockport has long cried out for a museum or cultural resource in the core of the old town centre. Staircase House, on the Market Place, could not be more central or more appropriate, presenting as it does the history of the town in its own fabric, from the time of the first merchant's workshop and house which was built on this burgage plot, fronting the Market, in about 1460.

At the time of writing it is due to open in late Summer 2005, when the interpretation of the merchant's house will be supplemented by Stockport Story, a museum next door, telling the more general history of the town. Since the nineteenth century the town's museum has been in Vernon Park, thanks to the generosity of two local MPs. Many have felt that a unique building in the town centre would be better suited to this role and Staircase House was suggested as far back as Victorian times. It was only after the efforts of a dedicated local group of heritage conservation enthusiasts in the late 1980s that this became a serious possibility. But more on this later.

Plans at present for Staircase House involve furnishing the various rooms in different period styles to lead visitors through the different epochs in its history,

The well-preserved seventeenth-century staircase was once the jewel in the crown of Staircase House until someone set fire to it.

with the help of a hand-held audio guide providing commentary. A sense of place will be created and personalised through dramatised stories of people who were involved in the events which affected the house.

The main phases of development covered will include its medieval origins, the Civil War of the seventeenth century, life in the kitchen and warehouse, elegant life in the eighteenth century when the 'blue dining room' was created, although bedrooms made use of the elaborate carved beds of the previous century, and then later uses of the building until the Second World War.

The front part of the restored Staircase House, re-faced in pink brickwork, was opened to the public as the tourist information centre in Summer 2004. It is open Monday to Saturday and provides a glimpse of one exposed medieval cruck blade, part of the medieval cobbles, the remains of a carved panel, and blackening caused by the unsuccessful attempt by some self-interested person to burn the building down in 1995. It makes my blood boil to think of how all the days months and years of selfless effort put in to save the building by dedicated volunteers could be jeopardised by the crass ignorance of one worthless fool.

Vernon Park and Museum

'On one round hill' is the name of the local history exhibition at Stockport Museum, charting the history of the town from the Stone Age. The Green Gallery brings environmental issues to a young audience with interactive specimen drawers. In the basement is an Aladdin's cave of treasures including porcelain, old photographic equipment and an ancient Egyptian mummy's hand. A window made out of crystalline Blue John stone is unique to the museum. There is a cafe next to the gun terrace with views of the Pennine hills. The museum is usually open from 1 p.m. until 4 p.m. and only at weekends in wintertime.

Vernon Park which surrounds the museum is Stockport's oldest park, opened in 1858 on land donated by Lord Vernon. It once boasted cannon captured in the Crimean War, but these were melted for scrap in the Second World War

Vernon Park on a 1900s postcard showing Pearsons Mill and old cottages near the road to Bredbury. The park was refurbished using a Lottery grant.

and replaced with replicas after the park won a Heritage Lottery grant in the late 1990s which returned many features to their Victorian splendour, including the bandstand, lily pond and water cascades. None of this might have been possible had it not been for the efforts of Roy Hampson, who single-handedly badgered everyone concerned into restoring the run-down park. He thought it possible when no one else did.

Vernon Park is worth visiting as an example of what one man can achieve. It is joined on to Woodbank Park, once the home of the mill-owning Marsland family, and boasts three way- marked trails – The Midshires Way, Etherow and Goyt Valley Way and the Fred Perry Way (whether '30s tennis star Fred Perry ever walked this way is another question). The River Goyt winds picturesquely beneath wooded banks and over two weirs, once providing water for the water tunnels which drove the early Stockport mill machinery.

Stockport Art Gallery

The Memorial Art Gallery opposite the Town Hall was built to commemorate the dead of the First World War in a classical Greek style and has an impressive sculpture of Britannia crowning a sacrificed youth next to the marble lists of war dead. The gallery has a permanent collection of mainly nineteenth- and twentieth-century oil paintings, watercolours, drawings and sculptures, including two L.S. Lowry's and some interesting 1930s ink and wash depictions of Stockport by Michael Conway. It also loans pictures and hosts contemporary exhibitions.

St Mary's Heritage Centre

On market days (Tuesdays, Fridays and Saturdays, 10 a.m. to 4 p.m.) St Mary's parish church, Market Place, is open to the public, as well as for services on Sundays and concerts at other times. Since 1999 a small volunteer-run heritage centre has been housed in the old vestry and choir room, with continually changing exhibitions on historical themes, including costumes and artefacts. It is run by enthusiasts from

The impressive tower of St Mary's church, which has regular services and concerts and houses Stockport Heritage Centre, run by local Heritage Trust volunteers.

Stockport Heritage Trust who collect the exhibits and present the displays with the help of donations from the kind people of Stockport.

If you have anything you think we might be interested in please pop in. Entry is free and there is a small souvenir shop and the chance to buy back copies of the popular *Stockport Heritage Magazine*. To date we have collected about 10,000 images of old Stockport, many of which are on display. We will also be mounting temporary exhibitions at Stockport Story Museum across the Market Place when it opens in 2005. Recently we have carried out research and site investigations for an exhibition on 'Underground Stockport' about the tunnels which riddle the soft sandstone beneath our feet.

Chadkirk Chapel and Country Estate

Situated in a broad, wooded section of the Goyt Valley, close to the Peak Forest Canal, just below the village of Romiley, the chapel, farmhouse and surrounding lands at Chadkirk are survivals of a medieval, or even Anglo-Saxon, landscape.

In the Domesday survey of 1086, 'Cedde', possibly Chadkirk, was described as a manor held from the Earl of Chester by Gamel, one of the few Saxons allowed to hold land after the Norman Conquest. 'There is a wood one and a half miles long and half as broad, a hedged enclosure and an airy of hawks and one acre of meadow. It was and is worth ten shillings. The whole manor is three miles long and one and a half miles broad.'

It is believed that some primitive monastic cell was founded here by St Chad, the Anglo-Saxon evangelist and Bishop of Mercia, in the seventh century. A 'holy well' on the lane leading down into Chadkirk Vale from Romiley is traditionally regarded as a place consecrated by the saint and is gaily decorated with a floral dressing every year during Chadkirk Festival at the end of July.

The old chapel contains early timber framework and is believed to date from the fourteenth century, although the earliest records refer to it in 1534, when Ralph Greene was the priest and the chapel was a chantry belonging to the Davenport family.

By 1621 William Webb, visiting this part of Cheshire said: 'At the foot of Werneth Low, towards the Mersey (now the Goyt), lies an old dearn and deavly Chappel, so people call desert places out of company and resort: called Chadchapell, where seems to have been some monkish cell.'

Later in the same century the chapel was used by the Independents for their meetings before they were ejected and, after lying derelict from 1706, it was restored by public subscription and Anglican services resumed in 1747. The adjacent farmhouse was also rebuilt at this time incorporating the timber framing of the original into the new design.

After the building of St Chad's in Romiley, services at the chapel declined and Bredbury and Romiley Council undertook some restoration to create a country park in the 1970s. This was considerably upgraded and a full archaeological survey was carried out in the 1990s, at the behest of Stockport Council.

Chadkirk chapel as it looked in the 1960s with a porch, before two extensive refurbishments. It has an enthusiastic Friends group.

A regular programme of concerts and activities take place and a resident warden keeps the farm and estate in good order, assisted by an enthusiastic Friends of Chadkirk group.

Chadkirk is approached on foot from the car park at the entrance to Vale Road and offers a rural heritage experience only a few miles from central Stockport.

Etherow Country Park

One of Britain's first country parks when it was established in 1968, with its deeply folded valley, broad Pennine vistas, woodland, lakes and waterways, Etherow is Stockport's most interesting park. Etherow estate nestles at the foot of Werneth Low, between Marple Bridge and Romiley. It was created to provide coal and waterpower for Compstall Mill, built by George Andrew in the 1820s.

The Keg was a shooting lodge for the Andrews, then a keepers cottage and the home of the first Etherow Park warden, John Hirst.

A massive waterwheel, the Lily wheel, drove machinery and coal was mined in the woods and brought by tram track across the River Etherow then along a canal by horse-drawn barge to the mill.

The estate now covers 240 acres, with woodland walks along the valley and up steep hillsides, past lakes and a spectacular stepped weir. The Keg woods and pool were the Andrew's own private shooting and fishing grounds. The owner is said to have boasted that: 'The earth is the Lord's and the fullness thereof, but Compstall belongs to Juddy Andrew.'

In 1817 he and his partners bought water rights to set up a mill and by 1824 the mill lodges, now used by Compstall Sailing Club and fishermen, had been built. Two early waterwheels were replaced by the massive Lily wheel in 1838. It had a 50ft diameter, produced 850 horsepower and was the largest in the country. A ten-hour day at Compstall Mills utilised forty million gallons of water which flowed through the mill via a series of water tunnels, now silted up. By 1840 steam engines were introduced and coal was being mined at a drift mine in Ernocroft wood, where the entrance can still be seen. Steam only took over completely in 1888 and the Lily wheel was demolished in 1906.

The company had built a model village to house mill workers. There was a church to improve morals, the Athenaeum, a public reading room, to improve the mind, and a company store to provide the necessities of life, to be purchased with the company tokens with which the workers, who lived in the company cottages, were paid. Rows and rows of these terraced cottages, now gaily painted, give Compstall part of its charm today.

In order to appreciate the village, turn off the main B6104 road, following the signs for the park. You will see the old building housing the post office and shop and a large wooden owl, carved from a tree stump, close by. Drive past this and turn right into the car park beside the visitor centre, cafe and lake. From here you can take a leisurely walk past the anglers as far as the weir. Beyond here, towards Keg Pool, or over the bridge into Ernocroft Wood, a sense of the old game preserve remains, with over 300 varieties of plants and 100 species of animals known to thrive. There are said to be mink hunting up and down the river, escapees from a mink farm and a danger to native animals. Red-spotted fungi sprout in the woodland, while dog's mercury, wood anemone, hedge woundwort and spotted orchids flourish in season.

Thanks to the farsighted enterprise of Bredbury and Romiley Council in 1965, the estate was purchased for just £5,000 from the Calico Printers Association. More and more land has been added over the years and it is possible to walk through to Broadbottom, with a slight diversion over Werneth Low – a walk with spectacular views. Guided rambles are organised by the wardens all year round.

Reddish Vale Country Park

A vital area of greenery in the Tame Valley between Denton, Reddish and Brinnington, this park covers 170 acres including mill lodges, used by fishermen, and home to waterfowl. The locally famous 'Sixteen Arches' railway viaduct in grey brickwork crosses the valley here. Superstitions warn it is unlucky to count all of the arches as they were cursed by a local witch! An old row of cottages once existed beneath them and it is rumoured that the old lady lived in one of the cottages and objected to the desecration of her beautiful valley by the railway. Now the viaduct is very much part of the scenery.

As a youth, along with many other local children, I used to bathe in the river here on sunny summer days. A sandy bank and pebbly foreshore acted as our 'beach' in a loop of the river on the Brinnington side and there was plenty of greensward for picnics. In those days the river was muckier than today – black and foamy – but there was an interesting old weir, with sluice gates which we precariously used to paddle over, now sadly disappeared. The lodges were full of coloured sludge from the printworks then and slimy oil slicks filled the access channels. I once remember having to rescue my dog from one of these; we were not very popular when we got home!

Stockport's butterfly park was developed on the site of the demolished printworks in a new herb garden and a warden-staffed visitor centre, with exhibits, regularly hosts talks and walks along the Reddish Vale Trail. Further along the valley between Bredbury and Haughton Green, the river runs briskly through a rocky sandstone gorge. Here are remains of Arden Cornmill, attacked by Luddites in 1812, and across the river in Denton Woods are the remains of ancient native woodlands including many oak trees, and home to rare reptiles.

Plaza Theatre Cinema

Saved by the efforts of a voluntary group, the Plaza in Mersey Square really deserves a visit from anyone serious about Stockport. It is an Art Deco-style building, reminiscent of a 1930s plain-tiled fireplace in its front façade, but with lovely Art Deco reliefs, lamps and plasterwork inside. There is also a unique, illuminated Compton organ in front of the stage, still in working order. The auditorium seems shallow, but it has a wide sweep and could originally seat

The 'nine houses' below Reddish Vale viaduct, with the royal train crossing in 1905.

nearly 1,900 people in the circle and stalls. Circle seats included the romantic couch-like two-seaters! The building is tall, having been built into the solid rock of the valley sides on a steel framework in 1932.

After the closure of the Davenport Theatre in 1997, Stockport was left without a theatre of reasonable size and when Plaza Mecca Bingo announced the sale of their building the following year, the Plaza Association was formed to try and save it as a theatre cinema. It attracted enthusiasts from all over, who set to stripping it out and getting it ready for productions once financial backing was arranged. I had a small part in ensuring its success when the whole project was put in jeopardy in 1999.

Today the Plaza, managed by Stockport Plaza Trust, hosts regular shows, concerts and films. Its pantomime is a popular local event and regular open days allow visitors to see the projection room and massive twin projectors at the top of the building and visit the dressing rooms backstage, where the stars prepare their grand entrances. Friends of the Plaza regularly help out, ensuring that the theatre is a truly local community enterprise.

Stockport Market

A market has existed here since Anglo-Saxon times, but the first market charter dates from 1260, and probably merely ratified activities which had been going on for some time. Local lord, Robert de Stokeport, established by the charter his right to rent for stalls and what his tenants could or could not do within his 'ville of Stokeport'.

Aikin described the market as 'spacious and convenient' in 1795 but it became so congested that Churchgate had to be widened to allow better access in 1818. In addition to the sale of animals and farm produce on Fridays (the cattle market was in Castle Yard) the market began to open on Saturdays by 1825. This was the day that mill workers finished early and got paid. Provisions were sold until 11.30 p.m. and the public houses around the market square did a roaring trade.

An ancient building used as a cheese and meal house stood at the west end of the Market Place, but it was so dirty it deterred dealers from attending the market. In 1824 it was bought by the inhabitants of the Market Place who had it demolished and a new cheese and meal house, also doubling as a courtroom and council chamber on non-market days, was erected at the bottom of Vernon Street – now part of the grand Courts development. The mayor, aldermen and magistrates were relieved to quit their normal meeting place: the dark cramped room above the old dungeon on Mealhouse Brow.

In 1850 Stockport Corporation bought the manorial rights to collect market tolls from Lord Vernon for £22,500. They demolished a timber-framed building which had been used as the town's post office and built the Farm Produce Hall or Hen Market with an imposing frontage in Classical style and a balcony from which official announcements could be made. Castle Mill, which became an inn, had been demolished in 1841 and the site was levelled still further for

Stockport cheesehall as it originally looked in 1852 with balustrades and stone urns, now removed.

St Petersgate Bridge – a street over a street in Little Underbank on an Edwardian postcard.

use as a cattle market. By 1861 the glass umbrella on stilts had been erected; originally open to the elements at ground level, the Market Hall was only enclosed after the stallholders petitioned for protection from the weather. Recently the Council thought about reversing this!

St Petersgate Bridge was built in 1868 to link the Market Place with the main approaches via Wellington Road and Edgeley railway station. The central section is cast iron supported by five brick arches spanning Little Underbank and creating one of old Stockport's favourite tourist views. The 'street over a street' bridge looks down on the famous chiming clock outside Winter's, with its figures of a soldier, sailor and Old Father Time, and a roofscape stretching away to St Mary's church tower, the Old Rectory and Robinson's Brewery. In the other direction, Little Underbank gently slopes towards the White Lion's black and white façade, Merseyway and the distant railway viaduct.

The market and Underbank, built along the valley of Tin Brook, grew up together and no visit to the market would be complete without a stroll along the Underbanks. Now hidden by shops, the sandstone bluffs on which the market stands gave Great and Little Underbank their names. They are still there, although you can't easily see them, and bits of old medieval masonry still cling in places. The black and white Three Shires bar was once the townhouse of the Legh family of Adlington Hall and the even more magnificent Underbank Hall, now a bank, was the Arderne family townhouse.

On the Market Place you can still see the Bull's Head from which radicals addressed the mob, the remains of the Angel Inn, haunt of Victorian street girls, the Packhorse, once the Vicar's courthouse and Staircase House itself. But more of this later. The market is open on Tuesday, Friday and Saturday all year and more often before Christmas.

Chapter 9

Stockport Heritage Trust

The idea for Stockport Heritage first matured in the wilds of North Wales. I say wilds advisedly, as my wife and I were then living in an old chapel house, once the home of a Welsh non-conformist preacher, but presently let out to any poor person who could afford the £10 a week rent. The house, draughty, damp, riddled with woodlice and perpetually shrouded in low cloud, huddled in a small hamlet on the edge of the Denbigh moors. In clear weather it had a fine, though distant, view of the crags of Snowdonia. It was surrounded by the incessant cry of bleating sheep. There was plenty of time to think.

I knew something of Stockport and its history and in particular Staircase House, having carried out research on the old market area. I had an idea for a heritage centre and wrote to the Council about it. They thanked me for my idea but at the time weren't too interested. Soon, work took me out of Wales and Bryn Myfyr (the name of the house means 'high study') first to London and then back to Manchester.

The idea for a heritage centre stayed with me and so on a summer day in 1986 my wife Jean and I walked into the Beehive Co-op in the old *Advertiser* building on High Street, Stockport, and met Iain McLean, an avowed community activist also interested in Stockport's heritage. He immediately took us upstairs to the old Labour club where we saw a councillor for the first time. 'Staircase Caff... 'eritage centre! Sounds orl right', said Cllr 'Bernard'. Thereafter, following this auspicious beginning, Bernard could be relied on to oppose us at every turn, for reasons known only to himself. Fortunately, he was out of step with the rest of his party.

We were on a political learning curve, which was to grow and expand over the next decade. In our simplicity we thought that well-meaning enthusiastic people, with a good idea and the know-how to make it happen, would be encouraged. But this was Stockport in the 1980s; there was rationing on enthusiasm and know-how was regarded with suspicion.

Our next step was a public meeting to launch Stockport Heritage Group in the Beehive Co-op, hosted by Iain McLean and addressed by Alan Edwards of the NW Civic Trust, who told us we had chosen the right moment to go for a heritage centre. Unfortunately Alan was to fall ill and die long before anything materialised – and that was the fate of many of our early helpers. But Jim Hooley, one of Stockport's oldest and best folk historians, was there and actually lived to see our heritage centre established in St Mary's church and work on Staircase House well underway.

Jean and I made some display panels about Staircase House using the resources at Manchester Polytechnic, where I worked, and borrowing photographs from Frank Galvin of Stockport Museum. Frank was eventually the man who would have the mammoth job of overseeing the restoration. We erected our first exhibition about our plans, and left leaflets I had made at our own expense, in Stockport Central Library. This drew the attention of Ron Gardner, one of the owners of Staircase House, who told us that the Council had served a dangerous building notice on him, with the advice that if the building were not repaired, it must be demolished.

To prevent the immediate demolition of the priceless fifteenth-century time capsule we had only just set about saving was our first task. We had T-shirts made printed with an old view of the viaduct and emblazoned with 'Stockport Heritage' which we sold to raise funds and wore en masse at vital Council meetings where decisions on the building's future were made. We lobbied councillors and MPs, talked to Council planners and English Heritage. We virtually lived in the offices of the *Stockport Messenger*, the *Express Advertiser* and other local media, keeping up a constant flow of updates on the unfolding drama. Jean started to hold a series of walks and talks on the subject of Stockport's heritage: the Market, Underbanks and Staircase House. I used to help her with the slide projector and heckle from the back with facts and figures she might stumble over! Fortunately one of these walks was recorded on audiotape and is now available as an audio CD.

We held a public meeting inside Staircase House and guided scores of people through the building, warning that it was at their own risk. Everyone who peered into the dusty wooden-panelled rooms, or mounted the ornately carved Jacobean staircase, or penetrated the rubble-strewn mullion-windowed cellar was enchanted by what they saw. Scores of restoration enthusiasts left that building – it was wonderful to see the effect it could have.

One Stockport Heritage member paid for a tree-ring dating survey of the oldest timbers, which placed the building back firmly into the medieval era – 1460 to be precise. Another found us Peter Hatfield, a brilliant architect, who crawled into dangerous spaces on his own to produce the first measured survey of the building, which proved that the original timber framework was at least 75% intact. English Heritage decided that Staircase House might be saved and offered grants to cover feasibility studies. Our volunteers never received a penny for their efforts – it was all done for love. In fact we very often paid for things with our own money.

Looking back, it is difficult to remember exactly why we did it. Had we known how long it would take to save Staircase House, which is finally due

Right above and below: The tattered upstairs rooms of Staircase House in the 1980s, with bowed panelling and collapsed ceilings.

Below: The staircase which climbed up three floors was still in quite good condition until the fire destroyed most of it.

to open to the public in Autumn 2005, I wonder how many of us would have persevered? We had applied for charitable status and I drew up a constitution which was approved by the Charity Commissioners. Theoretically we were in a position to raise funds for restoration, but without the backing of the Council, acquisition of the building was impossible.

In November 1987, just a year after Stockport Heritage was formed, Jean and I started *Stockport Heritage Magazine* with money I had saved from my job at Manchester Polytechnic. We had no idea how many issues could be published, or whether the first one would cover its costs. By selling it to thousands of local people we would promote interest in the heritage of our area and demonstrate to the doubters that there really was a groundswell of public enthusiasm. Even those people who were just spending 85p on a magazine were demonstrating their support. In the first year of publication, with issues in Winter, Spring, Summer and Autumn, and sales of up to 6,500 copies per issue, the magazine covered its costs and made a small profit of just over £600. Jean and I had to live on our £40-a-week enterprise allowance each, as the magazine and voluntary work for Stockport Heritage was a full-time occupation. I mention this, because it is important to know, if you are thinking of achieving a community enterprise against the odds, that this is the level of commitment it requires.

In the magazine we described the work of Stockport Heritage: a voluntary group formed to encourage the appreciation and preservation of historically valuable buildings, open spaces, traditions and anything of cultural value. 'One of our aims is the establishment of a Heritage Centre in a suitable building, where local people can meet, talk, study and where history can live and encourage a sense of place', we proclaimed. In the magazine's first issue we described our fight to preserve Staircase House and asked if this might be our heritage centre.

Through the magazine we made the area's rich fund of heritage material accessible to people who wouldn't normally read local history books and added to the interest by the lavish use of striking old photographs which provided a real window on the past. Vanished scenes could be transposed on familiar views of the present, creating a depth of historical perspective. We were also fortunate in receiving the contributions of some fascinating writers on local themes. Jim Hooley wrote about Hillgate, Edith Hinson, born in 1910, described her childhood around Newbridge Lane, Portwood and the old Market in an endless series of warm, earthy, articles all written by hand. Erudite scholars like Angela Phillips wrote of Stockport's early industry. We had a bountiful supply of material from ordinary people, all published if it was decipherable, and gradually the magazine evolved into a true community publication, written for and by the people of Stockport.

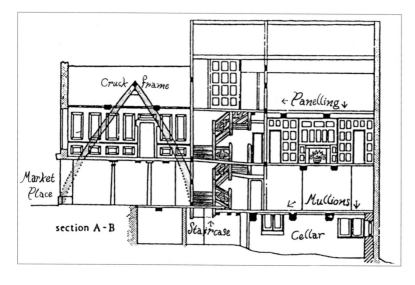

A cross-section of the building shows the cruck frame in the front, staircase in the middle and the upper panelled rooms, all of which are faithfully restored.

Generating public opinion became a full-time unpaid job for Jean and I, seen here showing the mayor and mayoress a copy of *Stockport Heritage Magazine*, with Iain McLean looking on.

Jean and I were kept very busy delivering and redelivering to newsagents, pubs, bookshops, garden centres – in fact anyone who would take the magazine. Jean also canvassed the adverts and did the invoicing while I handled the editorial side and drove the car. The magazine certainly made an impact – not all of it positive. Some cynical politicians in the Town Hall even suspected there must be big money behind the whole venture and grew suspicious because the magazine and our campaign was too good to be the product of 'woolly minded academics'. In truth it was actually put together by two idealistic amateurs on the kitchen table of a Council house in Brinnington, with kids wandering in and out asking for their tea! Neither of us were even clever academics: Jean's background was in sales and I was a journalist.

Stockport Heritage Trust was created when we gained charitable status in 1988. Iain McLean was our first chairman and was very supportive of the group's endeavours, utilising his contacts among the biggest political party on the Council to further our cause. We held regular meetings in the historic Arden Arms on Millgate, where everyone got a chance to air their views – some of them quite eccentric and not always very useful. One supporter, for instance, was a member of the Magic Circle, but he couldn't produce money from a hat! We found time to support other causes, like the campaign to save seventy acres of green belt in Reddish Vale which was going to be sold off. Jean and I were at the forefront of the march with our placards. We also successfully opposed a gravel pit in Woodbank Park.

Meanwhile our architect, Peter Hatfield, was arguing that our plans for Staircase House could act as a catalyst, enhancing the tourist potential of the Market Place and Underbanks and providing a turning point for the area. We were enthusiastically supporting any ideas for tourism in the area, like the opening up of the old air-raid tunnels on Chestergate, which were just being discussed, or the refurbishment of derelict Wellington Mill, then just a hope for the future. We supported the vicar and congregation of St Elisabeth's church

in Reddish, when the beautiful Alfred Waterhouse-designed building was threatened with closure. Time and again our intervention tipped the balance in favour of a heritage project, or to prevent a thoughtless act of environmental vandalism.

In 1989 the Council agreed to underwrite a loan from the Architectural Heritage Fund we had negotiated to try and buy Staircase House and start the restoration. We began fundraising and revived the ancient beating the bounds ceremony with a large festival in Woodbank Park and scores of volunteers in period costume helping to man stalls and organise the walk around the borough boundary. All the money we raised from this and other events went into a fund which is being donated to the fitting-out of Staircase House.

The Trust's efforts had, however, failed to acquire the building and Jean and I were concentrating on earning a living with another magazine venture in North Wales. An appeal from a Stockport Heritage member that 'the spark' had gone out with our departure brought us back. Seemingly all our efforts to save Staircase House so far had got nowhere. We broadened the appeal, arguing that European money could be used to upgrade the whole Market and Underbanks along with Staircase House, and got Euro MP Glyn Ford to back our ideas. That was in 1990, when the Council were using such grants to develop 'Kings Valley' – the first keystone of which was the blue glass pyramid, now a famous Stockport landmark. It was to be one of several pyramids which never got built. The pyramid became a 'white elephant', lying empty for years before the Co-op telephone banking service bravely took it on.

Scaffolding shrouds the front, rear and sides of Staircase House after the Council forced the owner to take remedial action, preventing imminent collapse.

In 1992 I joined Stockport Council for four years as an elected member, determined to win the support of all parties for the heritage of Stockport. I must have been the least controversial councillor in the history of the town, but by 1994 a planning brief was produced 'Towards a Centre of Attraction' in which all our arguments were used to justify retention and enhancement of the old town centre. Staircase House was to be the jewel in the crown of a major scheme, using regeneration budget money, and finally archaeological investigations began. A fire late in 1995 had concentrated people's minds and a massive bid for Lottery money was speeded up, before the crown lost its diadem.

Stockport Heritage has achieved many things in the interval. We established the annual medieval summer fair and re-enactment at Chadkirk. We instigated the blue plaques scheme, with the first to Judge John Bradshawe, near his birthplace in Marple. Members Phil Rowbotham and Stuart Peeres travelled to America and created the Dodge City Friendship link. Thousands of Dodge descendants in the US have ancestors from Stockport, and many visit Halliday Hill farmhouse in Offerton, one of their ancestral homes, in trips organised by another member, Ray Preston. Our heritage centre in St Mary's church was put together by Angela Conway, myself, Iain McLean and Jim Clare, with anything we could beg, borrow or donate. Again we did it with our own resources and a little help from our friends, including the rector Roger Scoones, without whose encouragement we would not be there. Jim Clare has developed the centre and collected many thousands of heritage photographs over the years. He also became chairman of the Trust after Iain McLean retired.

Jean never made it to see Staircase House open. She had a premonition that she wouldn't, but no one did more to save the place than her. She died suddenly in 1997 at an early age. Jean used to say: 'If you want something done, ask a busy person!' and she was busy to the end.

Sometimes I have difficulty remembering what it was that made the saving of Staircase House such an abiding obsession, but I think it was something to do with that sunny July morning in 1983, when Jean and I first mounted the time-blackened, ornately carved staircase and stood amazed in dusty panelled rooms carved by Jacobean craftsmen.

The place was in a mess – panelling was bowed out into the rooms, ceilings had collapsed, props held up beams and buckets were placed to catch rainwater coming through the roof. But there was such an atmosphere! For a breathless moment of discovery the centuries fell away in this secret corner of Stockport. It felt as if Bonnie Prince Charlie's lifeguards had just left on their flight from Government troops in 1745. Jean and I seemed to be transported back in time. We had discovered an archaeological opportunity, Stockport's equivalent of a temple overgrown and hidden in the jungle – a concrete jungle! We just had to share it with others and from this the idea for Stockport Heritage was born.

Now other young, enthusiastic people are caring for Staircase House. They are the professional staff of Stockport Heritage Services who work for the Council's museums. This unique survival of Stockport's mercantile development is being fitted out in different period styles to guide the visitor through from its early medieval beginnings to the last inhabitants in the 1940s. Other officers spent many years overseeing the complicated restoration process and keeping Stockport Heritage Trust onboard with the latest developments.

Why are organisations like Stockport Heritage important? Well, without them, many important opportunities for the expression and nurturing of local culture would be lost. Voluntary groups give an authentic voice to the

The fire-blistered panelling around the old fireplace after the arson attack. This has now been restored.

THE HISTORY OF STAIRCASE HOUSE

STAIRCASE House the 2ⁿᵈ graded building which was built as a farm house from trees felled in 1460 is probably Stockport's oldest building.

Yet it could so easily have been a different story if it hadn't been for the efforts of stalwart members of Stockport Heritage Trust, who recognised the value of the building to the people of the town back in the 1980s.

Steve Cliffe, its honorary secretary, and his late wife Jean *(pictured together at the house in 1987)* fought moves by the local authority to have the building demolished.

"Originally the council wanted to pull the building down and myself and Jean along with Iain McLean, our vice-president, established the group in 1987 and led the fight to prevent it from happening.

"We were on our own for a long time until we managed to get the Civic Trust and English Heritage to back our aims to save the building and eventually the building was listed.

"Staircase House embodies in its very fabric the ancestral heritage of Stockport. All those who visit this magnificent survival from other ages will feel a sense of awe."

When the building is completely restored and refurbished it will offer visitors an amazing opportunity to walk through rooms which will reflect its illustrious history through the ages from 17th century to the more gentrified accommodation of the early 18th century right through to the Second World War. Visitors will also see the 17th century kitchen and a warehouse. The huge amount of delicate

and intricate restoration work has been carried out by a team of between 60 and 70 expert carpenters, builders and craftsmen under the watchful eye of Donald Insall, the architectural firm responsible for the restoration of Windsor Castle after it was ravaged by fire. The workforce came from across the North West including Stockport and were employed by Linford Construction, a firm specialising in the restoration of historic buildings.

Coun Mark Hunter, the leader of Stockport Council, said the project which so many people had worked on to bring to

fruition demonstrated the local authority's commitment to the town centre.

He added:"The Staircase House restoration project will be a fantastic and most important achievement and I'm looking forward to seeing it in all its glory in due course."

Malcolm Cooper, the regional director for English Heritage said: "The people of Stockport have an extraordinary building in their midst, and a bit like an old friend, when it opens, it will be able to tell them about the development of the town from medieval times to the present day."

Steve and Jean Cliffe on the staircase in their campaigning heyday in 1987. At the time, saving the building seemed a very long shot.

aspirations of local people, unhampered by official dictat, or institutionalised notions of how things 'ought' to be done. In a healthy democratic society authority must always be questioned, but not merely in a purely negative way. Alternative views must be put forward that are practical and capable of achievement. This is what Stockport Heritage, a group of ordinary members of the public, came together to do.

There is a groundswell of interest in heritage and it's getting stronger than it has ever been, despite the flood of trendy historical television docudramas. People want that authentic taste. I believe this comes from a real sense of discovery – that 'breathless moment in time' Jean and I felt long ago in that dusty, neglected building. I hope you will share the experience with us in a resurrected Staircase House – a living memorial, a truly amazing window on the past. A priceless gift of our heritage.

The Old Town Centre

Start from the Old Rectory Hotel at the top of Churchgate, where a fine view of the rolling panorama of Stockport's roofscape and skyline greets the eye.

If you use the hotel car park, you will be walking or driving over the former pond which used to supply the rectors of Stockport with ice for their icehouse, still located within the grounds, in front of the neo-Georgian office block. This dates to the seventeenth century and is a vaulted brick-lined sump, sunk in the ground to preserve the ice from melting and intended for various culinary purposes. Rectors of nearby St Mary's church lived here from at least the 1640s, when we have a record of one of them, Edmund Shallcrosse, who spent his childhood in Staircase House, being ejected by the Puritans who were winning the Civil War hereabouts. Poor Shallcrosse had a fine library of 600 books, quite a luxury in those days! But probably connected with his work as the town's only schoolmaster.

The rectory in those days was a triple-gabled timber-framed affair similar to Underbank Hall in a map of 1680. It was rebuilt in brick in 1743, though some original timbers were reused in the new Classical style we see today. Rectors and even the Bishop of Stockport lived here until the 1950s. One rich Victorian rector, probably Canon Symonds, added a hexagonal, brick, single-storey billiard room which was replaced by the dining room conservatory when the building was converted to an hotel in the 1980s. Among its better-known inhabitants were the Prescots, father and son, both rectors at St Mary's and active magistrates during the town's turbulent early industrial history, and William Shippen, a Tory Opposition leader in the House of Commons from 1725- 42, who was born there. During the Second World War the Old Rectory was a billet, first for the Cheshire Regiment and later on for American army officers. All this is recorded on a blue plaque erected near the hotel reception desk by Stockport Heritage Trust and the subject of a live local radio broadcast by the author when it was unveiled in 1994. Go inside and have a look. It is to the left of the rear entrance door.

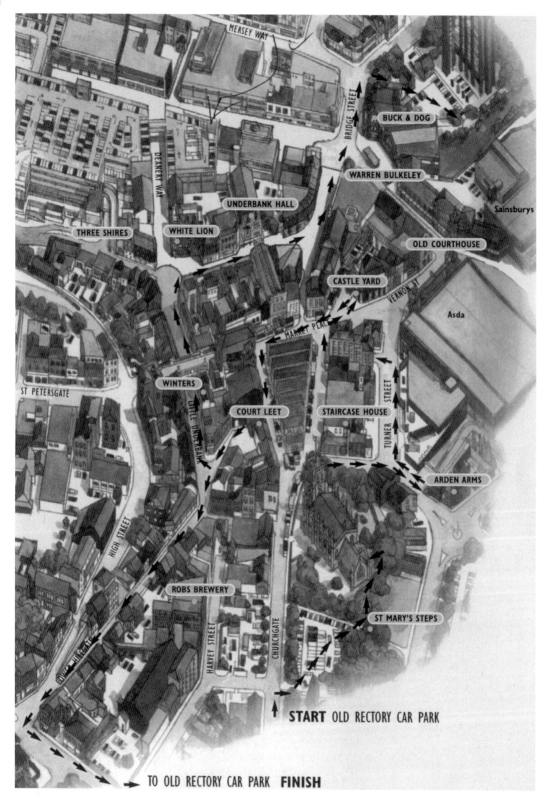

MERSEY WAY

BRIDGE STREET

BUCK & DOG

WARREN BULKELEY

Sainsburys

DEANERY WAY

UNDERBANK HALL

OLD COURTHOUSE

THREE SHIRES

WHITE LION

CASTLE YARD

VERNON ST

Asda

ST PETERSGATE

MARKET PLACE

WINTERS

LITTLE UNDERBANK

COURT LEET

STAIRCASE HOUSE

TURNER STREET

ARDEN ARMS

HIGH STREET

ROBS BREWERY

ST MARY'S STEPS

LOWER HILLGATE

HARVEY STREET

CHURCHGATE

START OLD RECTORY CAR PARK

TO OLD RECTORY CAR PARK **FINISH**

(Copyright SMBC, modified by Neil Winstanley, 2005.)

The Old Rectory on its hill above Spring Gardens showing the Victorian single-storey billiard room extension.

Exiting the Old Rectory via the front door you have a fine view of St Mary's church and a sweeping pathway leads you downhill onto Churchgate.

Just beyond the rectory gate before you reach the car park, an untidy bit of cobbled road branching right can be seen. This is all that remains of Loyalty Place, where Constable Birch was shot by McGhinness and nearly died. It once led to a large house in its own grounds on part of the hill which has fallen away, where it is believed the magistrate's clerk and Yeomanry officer John Lloyd resided.

On the left opposite the car park is a storage area once occupied by the Britannia Inn, an old half-timbered hostelry said to be haunted. Legends of vaults and wells beneath this area leading through to the old dungeon on Mealhouse Brow are told by people who claim to have explored them as children.

Head along the churchyard wall to the top of St Mary's Steps.

Here you can see how the church and graveyard sit atop a ridge while the river valley stretches away to the distant hills below. A stone plaque here records the Warren Almshouses, now demolished, and you are standing near the entrance to another 'secret' tunnel, now lost, said to access the church from the cellar of an almshouse via an ancient iron-studded door.

Enter the churchyard.

At the edge of the first sward of grass you will see a raised gravestone. This is a replacement for the original which lies beneath, recording the accidental death of Enoch Hill, a private in the local volunteer militia, 'killed by the bursting of a musket in the ranks' in 1794.

Near a small door in the red sandstone chancel is another raised tombstone with an iron railing. There is no decipherable inscription and it is a bit of a

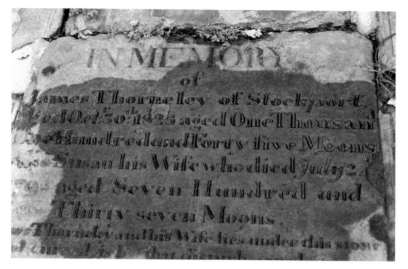

Above left: This mysterious moon grave gives the age in moons and contains a curse: 'Thorneley and his Wife lies under this stone and cursed is he that disturbs one bone'.

Above right: The last resting place of rector Richard de Vernon, near the old chancel.

mystery, but it may be the burial place of an ancient rector, Richard de Vernon, who oversaw the rebuilding of St Mary's in local sandstone in the 1300s. He was originally buried in a little chapel close by, now demolished, abutting the chancel door, but his remains were removed and some of his finger bones and teeth were taken as souvenirs and displayed at the Castle Inn, Market Place. His stone tomb effigy now rests in the chancel and a Victorian rector, Charles Prescot, ordered that the remaining pieces of de Vernon be given decent burial near the site of the old chapel in the churchyard.

Go around the back of the church to the north side.

A few paces from the railings around the steps to the boiler room is the moon grave. This records that: 'James Thorneley of Stockport died 30th October 1825 aged one thousand one hundred and forty five moons. Also Susan his wife who died 2nd July 1798 aged seven-hundred and thirty-seven moons. James Thorneley and his wife lie under this stone and cursed is he that disturbs one bone.' Well the bones may lie undisturbed, but unfortunately the gravestones have been rearranged at least twice since the 1970s in beautifications of the churchyard, the last of which, in 2001, involved the destruction of two lovely cherrytrees for a disabled ramp to the vestry doorway which never got built. Since then the curse seems to have worked as visitors hardly ever enter the heritage centre via the north door like they used to do!

If it is a market day and the heritage centre is open we can defy superstition and enter the old choir vestry. This is the main exhibition room of the centre set up by Stockport Heritage Trust and has a souvenir shop. In one wall is the original fourteenth-century Gothic doorway to the vestry proper, where priests used to change their vestments. It contains a charming oratory, a blocked stair to a vanished upper room and an old fireplace. The wall and ceiling panelling is early nineteenth century and the carved doors to the oratory are outstanding, though little is known of them.

The chancel has a long series of cruck frames, reputedly all fourteenth century, but some must have been replaced, or patched in sections. They still hold up the roof. There are some magnificent marble wall memorials and a few brasses. The effigy of Richard de Vernon can be seen just over the altar rail, recumbent in the Easter Sepulchre, which really should be empty as it represents the empty tomb after Jesus was resurrected.

Further down the church admire the stained glass which is mainly Victorian, as are the pews. Above the chancel arch are the arms of George III. There is an ancient pulpit with painted panels depicting the arms of local families arranged around the base of a stone column. A memorial to Charles Prescot, rector and magistrate, dominates the south wall of the nave. The upper galleries are extensive and now used mainly for storage, but give an ample view of the original organ pipes, although the present organ is electric. The church tower is ascended by a stone spiral stair past the bell-ringing chamber, the bells and the clock mechanism to the leads of the roof, with views through the parapet over the Market Place and beyond. The author enjoyed setting off fireworks from here and unofficially ringing the bells with a group of revellers on Millennium eve 1999-2000. Unfortunately, safety precludes this being included in the walking tour.

Leave the church by the west door in the tower and outside you will have a fine view of the glass Market Hall framed in the entrance archways to the churchyard.

Underfoot there are several Masonic gravestones with strange moon, star, ladder and compass symbols. Opposite is the Pack Horse pub, once the rector's ecclesiastical courtroom, formerly attached to an old black and white priest's house which was dismantled and re-erected as an aviary in Vernon Park in 1886. This was burnt down by vandals in the 1940s. It is believed that this gabled structure was the first priest's house and must have been standing before 1590. It was last used as part of Crossley's eating house and stood next to the old Dog and Partridge Inn on Rostron Brow. Both were removed to create 'a gin palace', the present rather tatty structure, now a shop, which would benefit from a lick of paint. I don't mean the Pack Horse, which is a pleasant old-fashioned pub with odd-shaped rooms, excellent bar meals and a pleasant landlady.

Stockport Heritage campaigned to upgrade this whole area back in the 1980s and early '90s and the work is still ongoing. First fruits can be seen in

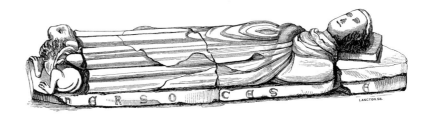

Effigy of Richard de Vernon who died 1334. His feet rest on a lion.

Old priest's house, Pack Horse pub and Market Hall viewed from the churchyard, 1880s.

The Old Golden Ball during restoration in the 1990s, where a prostitute was dangled upside down from an upper window.

the Johnnie Johnson Housing Association development at the top of Millgate, opposite the church. This was part of a plan to reintroduce town-centre living by providing affordable flats in new and refurbished old buildings. Ironically this street was once known for its prostitutes and, during the First World War, one was dangled upside down from an upper window of the old Golden Ball public house (now a part of these flats), her legs strapped together by a sailor's belt and his pet monkey tied to her waist. Apparently he had caught her trying to steal money from his trousers!

Go down Millgate (trying not to be run over by the cars shooting onto the car park ramps at Asda) and admire the Arden Arms pub built by the Raffalds in 1815 and probably the best-preserved old pub in Stockport.

In winter it has two open fires which add charm to the rich wood-panelled decor. The bar still has sash windows and old tiles grace the floor. Their Robinson's beer, brewed at the nearby Hillgate brewery, with Stockport water drawn from 600ft wells, is arguably the best in town and in the summer can be enjoyed in a delightful beer garden in the old cobbled yard where horse buses used to be stabled.

Head back up Millgate and go behind the restored black and white jumble of Staircase House while trying to ignore the ugly service yard of Asda – a legacy of a former regime at the planning department.

The interesting arched sub-cellar of Staircase House can be seen. Historians speculate as to its purpose – some favour the theory of a cool-room for storing cheese, others some industrial process as yet unknown. New buildings on either side provide easier access, including a lift, without damaging the original fabric. Stockport Story Museum occupies the refurbished Georgian building at the top of cobbled Park Street, but head for Vernon Street where you will see the restored Georgian Classical façade of the old courthouse and former police station.

Yet another cobbled brow leads onto the Market Place and we turn onto Castle Yard, now refurbished as part of the 'Courts' shopping development.

Cobbled Park Street will host the Stockport Story Museum.

Here stood the medieval castle on a mound. In the eighteenth century Sir George Warren built his early castellated muslin mill which later became the Castle Inn and provided an exercise yard for special constables, militia and Yeomanry during the industrial troubles. If you go inside TK Max you can see near the tills on the top floor one ceiling preserved from an old courtroom. The Council still has the Georgian benches and dock from one courtroom in storage somewhere.

Beneath your feet, several floors down and under tons of concrete, are the remains of the wheelpit and water tunnels which drove the muslin mill and the remains of a twelfth-century medieval well.

The Bakers Vaults by Castle Yard is an unusually shaped Victorian hostelry, famed for live music and with a singular bar, unchanged for years. It had a famous 'outdoor' on Bridge Street Brow where mill workers' wives would call for a jug of ale to take home nestling beneath their shawls. Beyond the Brow is the palatial produce hall, recently upgraded with an upstairs cafe. Next door are the interesting façades of the former 'building society block' and the remains of the Angel Inn, now housing Chafes solicitors' office. Internal walls here show timber framing and wattle and daub. A yard at the back, accessed behind the Town Warden's office, was a venue for brass band concerts and beef-eating contests in the good old days. If the gate is open it's possible to look over a wall down towards Underbank and see a section of the old medieval town wall, built of big oblong blocks of sandstone very like the walls at Chester.

A flight of steps known as the Devil's Steps goes down from near here. The story is that this was Stockport's Edwardian red light area and that one young lady danced with the devil on the steps, and he left his cloven hoof print as

The arched sub-cellar at Staircase House is a mystery to archaeologists and has yet to be fully investigated.

Interesting upper façades of the former building society block beside the Produce Hall conceal real timber framework from Tudor times.

Palatial interior of the former district bank, now a wine bar.

a calling card. Local children used to step on this to prevent 'Old Nick' from following them!

Over the road is the old district bank, now another bar, with fine granite columns and lofty ceilings. A little down the market facing the glass Market Hall is the Bulls Head, still a spacious pub, where Cobden, Chartists and radicals held meetings and spoke to swarming crowds outside, in what was then an open market area. The Council has its eye on opening up the Market Hall again, just over a hundred years since stallholder Ephraim Marks, of Marks and Spencer fame, petitioned to enclose his stall and the sides were filled in.

A little further on and the ground dips towards Mealhouse, or Dungeon Brow, one of the oldest routes onto the market. Ancient wooden pipes, made from hollowed logs, led drainage towards Tin Brook down here and it is alleged to be a Roman trackway. Extensive renovation of the old mealhouse by Northern Counties Housing Association has revealed the existence of five vaulted cells and extensive medieval walling on the site of the old dungeon and court leet room. Unfortunately the site is so unstable that the entire building very nearly collapsed and large portions of the medieval wall have been hidden by reinforcements. Some of the cells fill with water after rain and have no natural light. They would have been very dank and horrible places to be confined for even a short period. One is accessed by a spiral stone stair and has a hatch in the vaulted roof for lowering food or a lantern. They are believed to have been used until the early nineteenth century and thereafter for market storage.

If we descend Mealhouse Brow today there is little sense of how narrow and confined it used to be. Historians believe there may have been a rudimentary gateway here. Many people were crushed to death here when a firework display on the Market Place caused a surge in the crowd during celebrations for the opening of Vernon Park in 1858. At the bottom, near the junction of Hillgate and Little Underbank, stood the Sun Inn, where Jonathan Thatcher rode his cow as depicted in the eighteenth-century cartoon. The manorial bakery, where burgesses had to bake their bread in the lord's ovens, also stood nearby. There used to be access to a yard here where you could look up and view another part of the old town wall which once encircled the Market Place.

Heading down Little Underbank towards St Petersgate Bridge, we see an opening on our left into Royal Oak Yard, almost opposite Winter's wine bar and clock house.

The *Stockport Advertiser* building on High Street in the 1950s was a hive of activity.

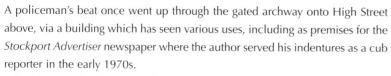

Above left: The cavern off Royal Oak Yard, once used to park *Advertiser* circulation vans, bears ancient handpick marks.

Above right: Staff climb the stone steps, once a policeman's beat, deep within the *Advertiser*, beneath an old gas lamp.

A policeman's beat once went up through the gated archway onto High Street above, via a building which has seen various uses, including as premises for the *Stockport Advertiser* newspaper where the author served his indentures as a cub reporter in the early 1970s.

I well remember Thursday afternoons when smoke from the bubbling vats of hot metal in the basement used to drift in through the windows of the reporter's room on the top floor, letting us know that the stereos (moulded half-cylinders of type) were being prepared for the presses. Later this laborious process would be replaced by web offset and then the amazing print processes of today. But not at the *Advertiser* – hot metal printed essentially the same newspaper for over a hundred years.

The cobbled yard was used by *Advertiser* circulation vans and their garage was in a rock cavern, excavated in the sandstone bedrock and still there in the bowels of the present building. The Royal Oak was a large half timber and triple-gabled inn on early maps. Bonnie Prince Charlie's Jacobite cavalry stabled their horses down here in Royal Oak Yard and Prince Rupert is said to have done the same a hundred years before. The long yard winds under part of Petersgate Bridge seldom seen and behind the Queen Anne, a very early pub. Here more caves can be seen, though much smaller than the ones under the old *Advertiser* building or the one where Turners Wine Vaults used to store their thousands of bottles of vintage plonk, hidden at the back of an old stable beneath the bridge. This was large enough for eighteenth-century freemasons to hold a candlelit banquet there!

The Tin Brook runs in a culvert beneath Royal Oak Yard and was responsible for carving the deep valley which forms the Underbanks after the last Ice Age. It is sometimes alleged that it got its name from the cave shelters alongside it being used by tin smiths in days when pots and pans used to be mended with this substance. The yard has an atmosphere and was used by Granada television in their dramatisation of the Dickens novel *Hard Times*.

Returning to Little Underbank, we can admire the fine clock with figures which move (when the clock is working) of a soldier, sailor and Old Father Time.

When I worked at the *Advertiser* the quarterly chimes of the bells, struck by the moving figures, was a charming feature of the area. Alas, since the jewellers moved out, a succession of wine bar licensees have failed to keep the clock in working order. Anyone wanting to see the mechanism can go upstairs to the public bar and if you are really unlucky they may let you wind the mechanism which involves weights and pulleys which go into the basement!

Jacob Winter was the jeweller who introduced the clock in the 1880s. He also had a hydraulic window display which could be lowered into the basement for security, powered by spring water. Since the jewellers left, clockhouse, as it is sometimes known, only regained a modicum of success by becoming a Holt's house and selling some of the cheapest beer in town.

Petersgate Bridge, opened in 1868, links the Market Place with St Petersgate and was intended to make access from Wellington Road and the railway station easier. It provides a picturesque cast-iron arch over Little Underbank and necessitated the alteration of the Queen Anne pub, which was sliced in half by it. The Queen Anne, or Queen's Head, which bears her portrait, has the smallest gent's toilets in Stockport. It also has a 'ghost room' at the top of a flight of stone steps and tiny panelled rooms reminiscent of a vanished age. The bar has a unique tap system of ivory and inlaid brass. It is said that artists and literary men of the town used to meet here and consume quantities of 'pungent punch' to 'mellow down their evenings'. Seven large murals by William Shuttleworth, a local artist, adorned the walls, but these have been lost or covered over.

At the junction of Great Underbank is the White Lion, once a low black and white-timbered building and possibly the oldest hostelry in the town, with a licence dating to the fourteenth century. It was a coaching inn, rebuilt in 1904 on a grander scale, in mock Tudor. Hillgate, leading down to Underbank, was the main coach route into and out of Stockport, heading, as it did, for the only crossing point of the Mersey at Lancashire Bridge. A cannon stood in front of the inn and was fired to let townspeople know when the mail coach arrived with important news.

In 1831 an incident occurred here which has been described in one of the novels of Thomas Hardy, when a man, William Clayton, followed the ancient folk custom of selling his wife to the highest bidder. She was handed over to the purchaser, J. Booth, for five shillings with a halter around her neck, as if she were a piece of livestock. It is not known if W. Clayton became the Mayor of 'Casterbridge' afterwards, or whether he regretted his action.

Turn left down Great Underbank and the black and white former townhouse of the Leghs of Adlington can be seen, now the Three Shires wine bar with its blue plaque.

Top: Winter's clock and the moving figures which rang the bells – once a regular sound in Little Underbank.

Middle: The Queen's Head, one of the narrowest and oldest pubs in Stockport.

Bottom: A wife was sold here at the White Lion in 1831 for five shillings.

The Leghs owned the land here, which stretched down to the river, from the fourteenth century. It is now truncated, but gives some idea of the typical form of Stockport houses in Tudor times. In late Victorian and Edwardian times it was a cake shop with a wine licence, 'Fowdens', where newly-weds toasted their happiness with sherry and Madeira cake.

Tin Brook crosses the road at its lowest point here and frequent inundations are due to debris blocking the culvert. The last serious floods occurred in the 1970s when waters from the brook were unable to flow into the Mersey and bubbled up through manhole covers. The river flows with terrifying force in times of flood, within feet of the top of a concrete barrier in the nearby service area beneath Merseyway. Back in Tudor times, Tin Brook was a pleasant stream which meandered past the old grammar school, a small oblong building which stood alongside it, enabling pupils, when not at their lessons, to fish from the windows!

Across from the site of the old school, below Pickfords Brow, is a spot now beloved of pigeons, with some bird-limed exposed rock below the bridge to the Merseyway car park. It was here that the town's medieval bear used to be kept in a railed enclosure known as the bear pit or hole. Bear-baiting was a common entertainment, when dogs would be set on the bear and bets taken. Although performing bears which did tricks had a higher life expectancy, their quality of life may not have been better. The bear slept in a cave, or caves, said to be higher up Chestergate. These may have been the ones later widened out to provide Stockport's underground air-raid shelters, the entrance to which you can see nearby. Thousands of people sought refuge here in the Second World War – I wonder if their sleep was disturbed with visions of a mangy old bear?

Cross back over the fine cobbled turning circle in front of the White Lion and continue towards Bridge Street.

On the left you will see a much better example of a Stockport Tudor mansion. Underbank Hall is the only remaining triple-gabled townhouse shown on the 1680 map. It probably belonged to the Arderne family of Bredbury and has a magnificent seventeenth-century fireplace in the banking hall, as it is now a branch of the NatWest. Only the front section is original, but it *is* original, including the staircase and resident ghosts, from floor to attic. Anyone can go into the ground floor and read that the Arderne family had a townhouse here from at least the fifteenth century, but permission is needed to see the other parts. The building was first purchased for use as a bank in 1824 by partners including John Kenyon Winterbottom, a local lawyer and former mayor, who embezzled his clients' money. He was found out, went on the run, was caught, transported to Tasmania, served his sentence, got a job as town clerk at Hobart and did it again! He commenced his second prison sentence aged seventy-eight, survived, and died at his home in Hobart aged eighty-three.

Pass the bottom of Bridge Street Brow and you will see the reconstructed façade of the Warren Bulkeley pub, now Laura Ashley's.

The Three Shires wine bar was once a townhouse of the Leghs and is close to a point where the river often floods.

Underbank Hall, purchased as a bank from the estate of the Arderne family whose townhouse it was.

Lower Hillgate in Edwardian times looking towards Robinson's Brewery.

This building faced Lancashire Bridge, which is actually hidden by Barclays Bank and modern shops built in the 1980s. Nevertheless, the oily Mersey still slides inexorably beneath, sometimes rushing, sometimes rolling, but always moving, as it has done without remission since the last Ice Age, probably 15,000 years ago. If you go behind Barclays you will be puzzled to see stone animals carved above a doorway. This is a bit of token 'conservation' from the old Buck and Dog pub, once occupying the site. Another fallacious bit of nonsense is the flood stone of 1799, once located down a flight of steps below the bridge, set into the wall of the pub to record the flood of that year. This is now in the wall of the bank, partly hidden by a parking meter and having no relation to the actual height of the flood, despite the inscription.

Look over the railing from the car park and across the river can be seen the arched outlets for water tunnels, now blocked with sand and debris. The tunnels fed waterwheels and later steam engines which drove the cotton machinery in Park Mills, once the biggest cotton factory in the world but now covered by Sainsbury's. This was also the site of an early silk mill and corn mill and before that a legendary battleground between Anglo-Saxons and Danes. Bones, reputedly of Danes, have been found over the centuries, some as recently as the early 1980s when Sainsbury's was built.

The water tunnels were dug through sandstone rock and still riddle the area beneath Sainsbury's and Asda, bringing the water from higher up the River Goyt along Newbridge Lane. Another local legend holds that French prisoners from the Napoleonic wars were used to help excavate the tunnels and that their skeletons, still in their blue uniforms with brass buttons, lie side by side in a line, in one tunnel somewhere beneath Warren Street.

I'll leave you here, with a choice of exploring Merseyway and the shops of Prince's Street, or ascending by lift or elevator via The Courts to Castle Yard and the Market Place again. I would prefer Bridge Street Brow, to admire the way the buildings climb steeply up and to savour the aroma of the fresh fish and game shop, with its open frontage, so reminiscent of the medieval shops of Stockport and their fresh produce of long ago. Or you may prefer to explore Hillgate,

The original Thatched House tavern, shown as it appeared in 1882, was the town's first dispensary for the sick.

retracing your steps via Underbank and past the bottom of Mealhouse Brow. A Christian bookshop, tattoo parlour and sex shop vie for trade here and higher up is Robinson's famous brewery, who have been brewing here since 1838. On the way back to the Old Rectory you may notice Hopes Carr, an area of run-down early silk mills in the valley, earmarked for redevelopment. Finally, notice the Thatched House tavern, just over the road from the Old Rectory's icehouse. It is on the site of Stockport's first dispensary for the sick, run by Dr James Briscall from 1792, in a much smaller black and white tavern which stood there.

River Valley Trail

Start from Vernon Museum, Vernon Park. (Note: Wear walking boots.)

Standing in front of the award-winning museum and looking towards the hills you can see Pear Mill, one of the last large cotton mills built before the First World War. Portwood, in the other direction towards Stockport town centre, was once full of cotton mills, but now only a remnant, notably Vernon Mill and Meadow Mill, currently remain, many having been demolished in the 1980s and '90s.

Set off through the park downhill, past the refurbished drinking fountain, down the steps towards the lily pond and join the Valley Way footpath which follows the River Goyt upstream from near the old weir.

Entrances to the old corn mill water tunnel run underground from here. Above, the river terraced walks criss-cross wooded slopes. Divert through Woodbank Park. After following bends in the river you will come to an overgrown area. This is the site of the silted-up Swan Pool, once a reservoir and the earliest source of drinking water for the town, provided by Peter Marsland the mill owner who owned Woodbank Park. Following the footpath beside the river you will see some outcrops of local red sandstone rock and on the opposite bank of the river, Bredbury, once past Pear Mill the hotel complex of Bredbury Hall becomes visible. This once belonged to the Bredbury family dating back to Norman times. The existing buildings contain stone portions of a late medieval building and a Tudor timber-framed barn.

Follow the river round the playing fields and past another old weir.

A dispute arose in the nineteenth century between the Marslands who lived in Woodbank Hall on the slope above the woods and the Howards, another mill-owning family, over water rights. Each vied to extract water for their mills

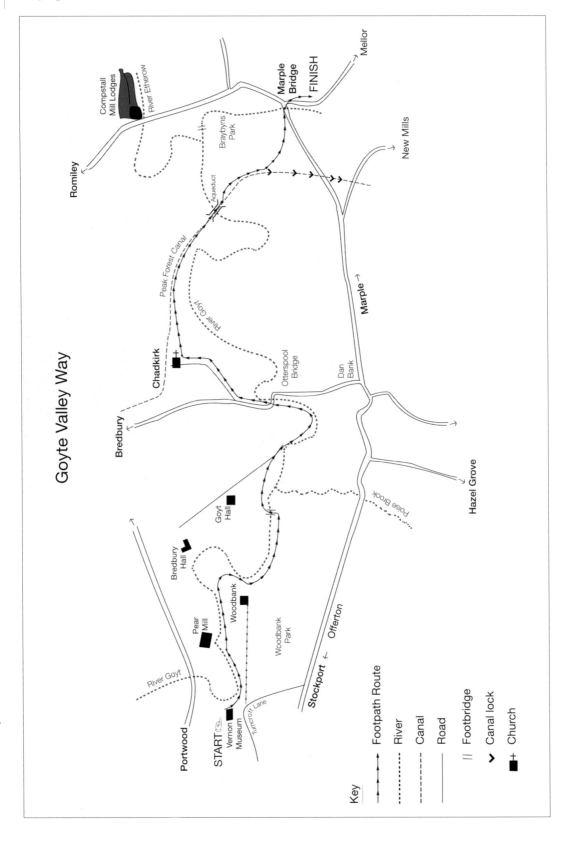

Goyte Valley Way

Compstall Mill Lodges

River Etherow

Romiley

Peak Forest Canal

Aqueduct

Braybyns Park

Marple Bridge

FINISH

Mellor

New Mills

River Goyt

Chadkirk

Bredbury

Otterspool Bridge

Dan Bank

Marple →

Goyt Hall

Bredbury Hall

Pear Mill

Woodbank

Woodbank Park

Poise Brook

Hazel Grove

River Goyt

Portwood

START

Vernon Museum

Turncroft Lane

Stockport ← Offerton

Key

→ Footpath Route

∙∙∙∙∙ River

--- Canal

—— Road

‖ Footbridge

➤ Canal lock

✝ Church

Pear Mill and Goyt Valley from Vernon Park in the 1950s. Werneth Low looms in the distance.

Goyt Hall Farm surrounded by fertile meadows and backed by woods.

from higher and higher up the river and tried to prove in court that the other was stealing their water!

The path goes up through the woods still following the river above a steep red sandstone cliff and is rather boggy here. There are wide vistas of the broad and fertile valley – once the main source of corn for baking bread in Stockport before grain was imported. Below us is an almost inaccessible cave known to local children as the devil's cave. Possibly early man may have utilised it. Stone implements have been found nearby. In the distance can be seen Middle Farm and the picturesque Goyt Hall Farm, a black and white structure with a duck pond, best viewed from the front.

The path skirts Woodbank running track then goes through woods to Woodlands Park, Offerton, descends past a cricket club and heads for Red Rock Fault and the Poise Brook through woods overrun with grey squirrels. The brook enters the Goyt along a clay and mudstone gorge which contains carboniferous fossils of ferns and ancient plants. The Red Rock Fault is a geological feature where the red sandstone of the Cheshire plain gives way to the grit stone of the Pennines, causing a rift in the valley. Just before the confluence, the Valley Way path crosses the River Goyt over the Jim Fernley footbridge and joins a track on the Bredbury side.

Further on this passes a pile of rubble, near the junction of a footpath to Bredbury Green, which is all that remains of Boggart House, once a farm labourer's cottage said to be haunted. 'Boggart' is an old English name for an unquiet spirit. In late Victorian times the house was lived in by an old labourer, a very religious man who worked for the author's great grandfather at Clapgate Farm. He would sing psalms in the fields as he worked to keep the spirits at bay! Earlier in the century the house was home to the notorious Oldham family, who terrorised the neighbourhood, robbing and committing violent assaults. One was transported and others were sent to prison.

Beside a stretch of river to Waterside Farm the remains of a millrace can be seen silted up. It was drawn from the weir, higher up near Otterspool Bridge, and was the final attempt by Jesse Howard, the mill owner, to take water from the Goyt for a new mill he planned at Warth Meadow, but it was never completed. Otterspool or Otterscow Bridge was a boundary of the northern limits of the old Royal Forest of Macclesfield. Towards Chadkirk is a ramshackle stone cottage set back from the modern road, which used to be the Stag and Pheasant. It was refused a beer licence because magistrates believed it encouraged tramps and undesirables like the Oldhams! The old road goes up through the woods from here, but we continue to Vale Road and Chadkirk chapel.

Turning down Vale Road we pass the entrance to Chadkirk Printworks, now industrial units, while over the fields can be glimpsed the bellcote of Chadkirk chapel on the site of a possible seventh-century Anglo-Saxon monastic cell.

Mentioned in the Domesday survey, it was probably an Anglo-Saxon manor and still has a remote other-worldly feel surrounded by its fields which include a perimeter farm trail. The farmhouse next to the chapel is Georgian, as is much

Below left: Chadkirk chapel, now restored and open to the public at weekends.

Below right: Otterspool Bridge and weir is passed on our way to Chadkirk.

of the chapel's present structure, but much older buildings once stood here. It is known that the Davenport's built the present chapel of timber, wattle and daub in the sixteenth century and the east wall is still timber framed. If it is the weekend the chapel should be open and you can stop here for refreshments and to admire the recently restored walled garden next to the churchyard.

Next head into the woods and follow a steep path from the churchyard towards the Peak Forest canal.

This skirts the grounds of Oakwood Hall, built in revivalist Tudor style in 1845 for Ormerod Heyworth, the owner of Oakwood Mills. Sadly it is now truncated after years of dereliction and former use as a school and monastery! Gaining the canal towpath you will shortly come to the start of the Hyde Bank tunnel,

Oakwood Hall had a grand view over the valley. It was later used as a school until the 1960s, when it lay empty and derelict.

Hyde Bank House was bought by Samuel Oldknow to use the land for his canal scheme.

AQUEDUCT AND VIADUCT, MARPLE.

A breathtaking view of the aqueduct and viaduct crossing the wooded Goyt Valley between Marple and Romiley.

near the gatehouse to Oakwood Hall. Bargees used to propel their boats by 'legging it' through here while the horse walked round. Follow the signs for Marple Aqueduct past Hyde Bank House, the former property of canal builder Samuel Oldknow. Regaining the canal path near the tunnel mouth you are above a series of bends in the River Goyt below, where Manchester Canoe Club practice their strokes.

After a short while you will walk onto Marple Aqueduct, with views of the wooded ravine of the Goyt and the railway viaduct.

The aqueduct was the civil engineering feat of its day and a hotel put up sightseers at the Marple end from the 1800s. It is 100ft above the river, but the viaduct is 24ft higher and was completed in 1862.

Carry on towards Marple and cross to the left-hand towpath.

Above left and right: Town Street collapsed into the Goyt and was replaced by this fine promenade above the river in 1992.

You will pass a series of beautiful locks and lock basins, which impound water to enable the locks to work. Take the footpath signed for Brabyns Park and Marple Bridge. After crossing the railway line by the footbridge and walking through the woods, wide playing fields appear. Near the car park and nursery stood Brabyns Hall, once the home of Elizabeth Brabyn, an heiress said to haunt the now vanished Marple Hall after an unhappy marriage to one of the Bradshawe Isherwoods. It was in use as a military hospital during the First World War but later demolished and the Park taken over by Marple UD Council. Plants are on sale in the nursery and there are pleasant walks alongside the Goyt.

Walk towards Brabyns Brow, past the lily pond, and, joining the main road, cross the bridge over the Goyt. Be careful crossing this busy road.

The swirling waters of the Goyt reflect sunlight as they pour over the remains of the old cornmill weir, below the promenade in Marple Bridge.

You are now in the picture postcard village of Marple Bridge. This was once in Derbyshire and part of the manor of Glossop owned by the monks of Basingwerk Abbey! Now, Town Street boasts a promenade, created after the road fell into the river in the early 1990s. Here you can again seek refreshments in one of several pubs or the cafe. It is a charming spot, with views of the rushing river over the wall, which once turned the wheel of a cornmill. It's possible to catch a bus back to Stockport from here, or you could go on to Roman Lakes along the unmade Low Lea Road, past Oldknow's orphanage. But I'll leave that to another day.

Bibliography

Aiken, J., *A Description of the Country from Thirty to Forty Miles Round Manchester* (1795)

Arrowsmith, P., *Stockport a History* (SMBC and GMAU, 1997)

Ashmore, O., *The Industrial Archaeology of Stockport* (Uni. of Manchester, 1975)

Astle, W., *Stockport Advertiser Centenary History of Stockport* (Swain & Co. Ltd, 1922)

Butterworth, J., *A Description of the Parish of Stockport* (1827)

Earwaker, J., *East Cheshire* (2 vols), (1877/80)

Galvin, F., *Stockport Town Trail* (SMBC, 1986)

Hearle, A., *Marple and Mellor* (Chalford Publishing, 1997)

Heginbotham, H., *Stockport Ancient and Modern* (2 vols), (1882/92)

Middleton, T., *Annals of Hyde and District* (1899)

Nevell, M., *Tameside* (4 vols 1991/94), (Tameside MBC and GMAU)

Ormerod, G., The History of the County Palatine and City of Chester (3 vols) (1882)

RCHM Historic Building Report, Staircase House (1993)

Reeves, E. and Turner, J., *Bredbury* (SMBC, 1991)

Stockport Heritage magazine (5 vols) (1987/2005)

Stockport official guide (SMBC, 2004)

Wainwright, J., *Memories of Marple* (1899)

Watson, Revd J., 'A manuscript collection towards a history of Cheshire' (*c.* 1780), Mss copy Stockport
Local Heritage Library.

Index